FAVORITE BRAND NAME™
BEST-LOVED
Italian

Publications International, Ltd.

Favorite Brand Name Recipes at www.fbnr.com

Inset photography of Italy on pages 5 upper right, 96, 130, 224, 234 and 238 by Cynthia M. Colby; pages 7, 8, 22, 38, 68, 80, 142, 150, 154, 160 and 210 by David Darian; pages 172, 188 and 208 by Ruth Siegel.

Pictured on the front cover: Shrimp Scampi *(page 158)*.
Pictured on the jacket flaps: Tomato and Caper Crostini *(page 26)* and Classic Anise Biscotti *(page 222)*.
Pictured on the back cover *(left to right):* Margherita Panini Bites *(page 18),* Baked Italian Meatballs *(page 90)* and Gramma's Cannoli Cassata *(page 228).*

ISBN-13: 978-1-4127-2576-7
ISBN-10: 1-4127-2576-3

Library of Congress Control Number: 2007921112

Manufactured in China.

8 7 6 5 4 3 2 1

Microwave Cooking: Microwave ovens vary in wattage. Use the cooking times as guidelines and check for doneness before adding more time.

Preparation/Cooking Times: Preparation times are based on the approximate amount of time required to assemble the recipe before cooking, baking, chilling or serving. These times include preparation steps such as measuring, chopping and mixing. The fact that some preparations and cooking can be done simultaneously is taken into account. Preparation of optional ingredients and serving suggestions is not included.

Contents

Best-Loved Italian Cooking

Ask anyone to name their favorite ethnic cuisines and Italian cooking is sure to be among their top choices. Spaghetti and meatballs, pizza and lasagna are such an important part of our culture that we often think of them as American dishes. If you haven't already discovered, Italian recipes are some of the easiest to make at home. *Best-Loved Italian Recipes* is filled with dozens of traditional favorites, such as fettuccine Alfredo, risotto, bruschetta, veal parmigiana, chicken piccata, shrimp scampi and tiramisù. You'll also find many contemporary Italian recipes that you'll soon add to your family's list of favorites. A few even have a delightful American spin. Best of all, most of the recipes are easy to prepare and use readily available ingredients. Some recipes call for ingredients that may only be available in large urban areas or in specialty food markets, but they are worth seeking out.

If you're not familiar with Italian ingredients, see pages 7–15 for a glossary of Italian food terms.

Italian Cuisine

The best food in Italy is often found in small family-owned trattorias and home kitchens. Traditional recipes have been passed down from generation to generation, often with each cook adding her own distinctive touch. Each region of the country has its traditional recipes and the cuisine in each region has been influenced by both geography and history. Geography and climate helped determine what crops grow best in each region; the abundance of local produce and livestock helped drive the creation of regional cuisines. For example, lasagna is a traditional Italian dish, but many versions exist. Besides regional differences in recipes, families often have their own special twist on this traditional dish. History played an important part too, especially in regions that were once part of another country or regions that were subjected to invasions from other countries. The Friuli-Venezia Giulia region in northeast Italy has been a part of Austria, Hungary, Germany and Yugoslavia;

after World War I it briefly became a part of Italy. In 1963 it became a permanent region of Italy. Among the favorite foods of this region that reflect its history are sauerkraut, goulash and strudel. In the case of invaders, often bits and pieces of their cuisine were left behind. Sicily is a perfect example. This island, located just off the southern tip of Italy, has been ruled at one time or another by the Greeks, Romans, Arabs, French and Spanish. Today's Sicilian cuisine includes Greek and Arab herbs and spices and French- and Spanish-style sauces. Arabs also brought rice, citrus fruit, dates, chickpeas and couscous. And tomatoes, so prized today throughout southern Italy, were introduced by the Spanish.

Italians have a great respect for food and consider mealtime almost sacred. Cooks take great pride in serving simple dishes that allow the ingredients to shine. Many still shop daily for the freshest locally grown vegetables and fruit; cooks favor ingredients at the peak of their growing season. Meat and poultry raised nearby, freshly caught seafood and fresh seasonal produce are the basis for the delicious dishes on family menus.

Regional Cuisines ❦

Some basic differences exist between the cuisines of northern and southern Italy. Cream-based sauces, butter, beef, veal, poultry and polenta are favored in the north, while tomato-based sauces, olive oil, sheep's and goat's milk cheeses, pizza, artichokes and hot peppers are common in the south. A list of ten of the most influential regions, their common foods and a few of their traditional dishes follows:

NORTHERN ITALY

Region
Emilia-Romagna
Main Cities
Bologna, Parma
Common Ingredients
Pork, seafood, Parmigiano-Reggiano cheese, wheat, balsamic vinegar
Traditional Dishes
Bolognese sauce, lasagna verdi, stuffed pasta, tortellini en brodo

Region
Friuli-Venezia Giulia
Main Cities
Trieste, Udine
Common Ingredients
Prosciutto, sausage, seafood, ricotta cheese, beans, cabbage
Traditional Dishes
Beef goulash, fish chowders, stuffed strudel, sauerkraut

Region
Lombardy
Main Cities
Como, Milan
Common Ingredients
Beef, veal, cream, butter, Gorgonzola cheese, mascarpone cheese
Traditional Dishes
Osso buco, panettone, risotto, veal with tuna sauce, minestrone, pork and cabbage stew, tripe soup

Region
Tuscany
Main Cities
Florence, Lucca, Pisa, Siena
Common Ingredients
Beef, seafood, olive oil, bread, cannelloni beans, chickpeas, fava beans, spinach, rosemary, barley
Traditional Dishes
Bruschetta, panzanella, panforte, spinach gnocchi, bean soup, risotto, lemon chicken

SOUTHERN ITALY

Region
Basilicata
Main Cities
Maratea, Matera, Potenza
Common Ingredients
Lamb, sheep's and goat's milk cheeses, pasta, bell peppers, eggplant, potatoes, tomatoes, zucchini, hot peppers
Traditional Dishes
Fusilli with ricotta, lasagna with beans, roasted lamb with vegetables

Region
Calabria
Main Cities
Catanzaro, Cosenza
Common Ingredients
Pork, seafood, pasta, bread, beans, bell peppers, citrus fruit, eggplant, figs, tomatoes, olives
Traditional Dishes
Eggplant dishes, pasta with vegetable sauce, peperonata, stuffed figs

Region
Campania
Main Cities
Naples, Salerno
Common Ingredients
Lamb, pork, poultry, seafood, mozzarella cheese, ricotta cheese, provolone cheese, mascarpone cheese, eggplant, figs, grapes, lemons, potatoes, tomatoes, hazelnuts
Traditional Dishes
Calzoni, pizza, spaghetti with meat sauce, stuffed eggplant

Region
Lazio
Main Cities
Latina, Rome, Tivoli
Common Ingredients
Lamb, pecorino Romano cheese, olive oil, pasta, rice, artichokes, arugula, gelato
Traditional Dishes
Lamb with rosemary, saltimbocca, spaghetti alla carbonara, stewed oxtail, pasta e fagioli, pasta with ricotta cheese, penne all'arrabbiata

Region
Sicily
Main Cities
Marsala, Messina, Palermo
Common Ingredients
Lamb, seafood, olive oil, pasta, couscous, gnocchi, bell peppers, citrus, dates, tomatoes, pistachio nuts, almonds, marsala wine
Traditional Dishes
Cannoli, caponata, cassata, meatballs in tomato sauce, peperonata

Region
Umbria
Main Cities
Assisi, Perugia, Spoleto
Common Ingredients
Beef, pork, prosciutto, pancetta, salami, olive oil, pasta, polenta, lentils, black truffles
Traditional Dishes
Minestrone, onion soup, porchetta, risotto with truffles, roasted pigeon

GLOSSARY

Al dente: The literal translation of this phrase is "to the tooth." It indicates a degree of doneness when cooking pasta—slightly firm and chewy, not soft.

Amaretti: Light, crisp almond-flavored macaroons available in specialty food markets, amaretti are often dipped into coffee or sweet wine and sometimes used in baking recipes.

Amaretto: An almond-flavored liqueur made from the kernels of apricot pits, amaretto is often used to flavor baked goods; it originated in Saronno, Italy.

Antipasto: An Italian term literally translated as "before the pasta," antipasto refers to an appetizer. A selection of appetizers (antipasti) may include sausage, cheese, olives and marinated vegetables.

Arborio Rice: A short-grain Italian rice high in starch, arborio is favored for making risotto because it produces a creamy texture.

Arugula: Popular in Mediterranean cuisines, arugula is a somewhat bitter salad green with a spicy, mustard-like flavor. It can be added to salads or soups and pairs well with beef.

Balsamic Vinegar: This aged vinegar is made from a variety of white grapes. The long aging process (10 to 25 years) mellows the vinegar and gives it a sweet, pungent flavor. Mass-produced balsamic vinegar has a sharper flavor because it is not aged as long as finer vinegars. Always buy the best quality balsamic vinegar you can afford.

Biscotti: These traditional Italian cookies come in many flavors but the classic is anise. They are crisp and crunchy as a result of double baking and are ideal for dipping into coffee or dessert wine.

Bistecca: Bistecca is the Italian word for "beef steak."

Bolognese, alla: Literally translated, alla Bolognese means "in the style of Bologna." Bologna is noted for rich, meaty sauces. Bolognese sauce is best known in America as a pasta sauce made with beef or veal, finely diced vegetables, wine and cream.

Braciola: This Italian term refers to a thin slice of meat wrapped around a filling and braised; the French call it a roulade.

Bresaola: Aged boneless beef that has been salted and air dried, bresaola has a mild, sweet flavor. It is often served as part of an antipasto selection or as a pizza topping.

Brodo: Brodo is the Italian term for "broth."

Bruschetta: This Italian term refers to bread that has been sliced, rubbed with garlic, toasted, then drizzled with olive oil. This toasted bread is often topped with tomatoes or other simple toppings, such as sautéed mushrooms, roasted red bell pepper or cooked eggplant, and served as an appetizer.

Cacciatora, alla: This term refers to dishes prepared "hunter's style." Cacciatore is the American spelling. The most popular dish is pollo alla cacciatora, in which chicken pieces are cooked in the oven or on top of the stove in a sauce of tomatoes, onions, garlic and mushrooms.

Caffè: Caffè is the Italian word for "coffee."

Calamari: Calamari is the Italian word for "squid." Fried calamari is a common dish in restaurants in both Italy and America.

Calzone: This half-moon-shaped pizza turnover originated in Naples where it was sold as street food. The plural is calzoni.

Campanella: A bell-shaped pasta, campanella has fluted edges and hollow centers, which are ideal for holding sauce.

Cannellini Beans: Mild-flavored white kidney beans, cannellini beans are the traditional beans in pasta e fagioli (pasta and bean soup).

Cannelloni: Cannelloni is a dish made from large tubes of pasta that are cooked, stuffed with meat or cheese, then baked in a sauce.

Cannoli: This traditional dessert is made with deep-fried tube-shaped pastry shells that are filled with a rich mixture of whipped, sweetened ricotta cheese, candied fruit, chocolate bits and sometimes chopped pistachio nuts.

Capelli d'Angelo: This is the Italian term for angel hair pasta.

Capers: Capers are deep green flower buds of a Mediterranean bush; the buds are preserved in a vinegary brine. Capers have a piquant, slightly bitter taste. They are used in salad dressings, as a condiment and in sauces for meat and seafood. They can be rinsed in cold water before using to remove excess brine.

Caponata: This traditional Sicilian dish is a cooked mixture of diced eggplant, onion, tomatoes, olives, capers and vinegar. Pine nuts and anchovies are also common ingredients. Caponata is most often served as a condiment in Italy or in America as an appetizer.

Cappelletti: Similar in shape to ravioli, cappelletti are small squares of pasta stuffed with meat or cheese, then shaped to resemble small three-cornered hats.

Cappuccino: A coffee drink made from espresso and topped with foamy steamed milk, cappuccino is served in a standard-size or large cup and topped with a dusting of cocoa powder or grated chocolate.

Carbonara: Carbonara refers to a traditional Roman pasta dish. A mixture of beaten eggs, cream, Parmesan cheese and cooked pancetta is tossed with piping hot pasta (usually spaghetti) for several minutes until the heat of the pasta thickens the sauce.

Carpaccio: Thinly shaved raw beef with a simple dressing of mayonnaise or olive oil and lemon juice, carpaccio is served as an appetizer.

 **Cassata:** This rich Italian dessert combines sponge cake soaked in liqueur and filled with a mixture of sweetened ricotta cheese, candied fruit and fine bits of chocolate. The dessert may also be layered in a dish.

Cavatelli: A type of pasta with a shell-like appearance, cavatelli is 1 to 2 inches in length with the long sides rolled inward.

Ciabatta: An open-textured, chewy country bread, ciabatta is a somewhat flat, oval loaf dusted with flour.

Conghiglie: A pasta shaped somewhat like a small conch shell, conghiglie is often used in pasta salads or served as a main dish with various sauces.

Crostini: Crostini refers to small thin slices of bread drizzled with olive oil and toasted; the term also refers to an appetizer of crostini with various toppings.

Ditali: A short (about ½ inch) narrow tube of pasta, ditali (also called ditalini) is a favorite addition to soups.

Dolce: The Italian term dolce means "sweets." It can also refer to sweet wines.

Escarole: A pale leafy green with a slightly bitter flavor, escarole is one of the featured ingredients in bean and escarole soup.

Espresso: Espresso, a very strong coffee served in small cups, is prepared in a special espresso maker under steam pressure, using finely ground Italian-roast beans. It is the base for other coffee drinks, such as cappuccino, caffè latte (espresso with hot milk) and caffè macchiato (espresso with a little steamed milk).

Farfalle: Farfalle is the Italian term for "bow-tie pasta."

Fava Beans: Large, flat, tan beans that resemble lima beans, fava beans are available canned, dried and fresh. They are a popular ingredient in Italian soups.

Fennel: Fennel or sweet anise is a bulbous vegetable with short, white to pale green stems and green feathery tops. Known as "finocchio" in Italian, fennel has a crisp texture and a slightly sweet licorice-like flavor that mellows when cooked.

Fiorentina, alla: This term means "in the style of Florence," referring to serving food on a bed of cooked spinach.

Firènze, alla: This Italian term means "in the style of Firènze," which is the Italian name for the city of Florence.

Focaccia: Focaccia is the Italian term for a thin, chewy, rustically shaped Italian flatbread that originated in Genoa. It is traditionally brushed with olive oil and sprinkled with salt before baking, but now can be found with a variety of toppings such as herbs, sun-dried tomatoes, garlic, onions and vegetables. Often served as an appetizer or a meal accompaniment, focaccia is also popular for sandwiches in America.

Formaggio: Formaggio is the Italian term for "cheese."

Fra Diavolo: Literally translated as "brother devil," fra diavolo refers to a hot, spicy sauce that always includes hot chili peppers and most often tomatoes. The sauce is frequently paired with pasta or seafood.

Frittata: Frittata is the term for a round Italian omelet in which the eggs are combined, before cooking, with other ingredients, such as meat, vegetables and herbs. The egg mixture is cooked slowly over low heat in a heavy skillet without stirring until it is set. A frittata can be served hot or cold. It is cut into wedges before serving.

Funghi: Funghi is the Italian word for "mushrooms."

Fusilli: A spiral-shaped strand of spaghetti, fusilli can be cut into any length, but 1-inch lengths are most common.

Gelato: Gelato is the Italian word for "ice cream." Gelato has a custard base and is generally denser in texture than American ice cream; fruit flavors are common.

Gemelli: A type of pasta created by braiding two strands of spaghetti together, gemelli is cut into short lengths.

Gnocchi: Italian for "dumpling," gnocchi are generally made from cooked potatoes, flour, and sometimes eggs and cheese. Gnocchi dough is shaped into small balls or squares and simmered in water.

Gorgonzola: Italy's version of blue cheese, Gorgonzola is made from cow's milk. Many believe it got its name from a town outside of Milan in Lombardy.

Granita: The Italian term for "ice," granita is a frozen mixture of sugar, water and flavorings, such as fruit juice, coffee or wine. It has a granular texture.

Gremolata: A simple mixture of grated lemon peel, finely chopped parsley and minced garlic, gremolata is traditionally served as a condiment with osso buco.

Manicotti: The term manicotti refers to the dish prepared by stuffing cooked manicotti pasta shells with a meat or cheese filling, then baking them in a sauce.

Marsala: Marsala is a fortified wine (additional alcohol is added to it) produced in Sicily. The dry version is usually offered as a before-dinner drink, while the sweet version is served after dinner and used to flavor desserts. Zabaglione, the traditional Italian light custard, is flavored with marsala.

Mascarpone: A rich, buttery soft cheese made from cow's milk, mascarpone is produced in the Lombardy region. It pairs well with fruit and is often an ingredient in desserts.

Milanese, alla: Meaning "in the style of Milan," meats and poultry prepared alla Milanese are dipped into beaten egg and coated with a mixture of dry bread crumbs and grated Parmesan cheese before panfrying in butter.

Minestrone: A traditional Italian hearty vegetable soup, minestrone often includes pasta and beans as well as vegetables. The  name comes from a derivation of the Italian term, minestra, meaning "soup."

Orecchiette: A small shaped pasta, orecchiette literally translated means "little ears."

Orzo: Orzo is a rice-shaped pasta that can be substituted for rice in soups or served as a main-dish accompaniment.

Osso Buco: A traditional Lombardy dish of veal shanks braised in a rich tomato sauce, osso buco is served with gremolata.

Parmigiana, alla: This term refers to dishes prepared "in the style of Parma" with Parmesan cheese and prosciutto. The American term, parmigiana, usually refers to dishes made with Parmesan cheese or a dish of meat or eggplant coated in bread crumbs, panfried and topped with tomato sauce, mozzarella and Parmesan cheeses.

Parmigiano-Reggiano Cheese: The most famous of the Italian Parmesan cheeses, Parmigiano-Reggiano, produced mostly in Parma, Bologna and Modena, is aged longer than other Parmesan cheeses for a more complex flavor.

Pancetta: Pancetta is Italian bacon; unlike American bacon it is not smoked, but rather cured with salt and spices. It comes in round rolls and is often sold sliced and packaged.

Panettone: A Christmas or Easter favorite, panettone is a yeast-raised anise-flavored cake made with raisins, candied citron and nuts. It is usually a cylindrical shape.

Panforte: A dense cake loaded with candied citron, nuts and flavored with cocoa and spices, panforte is served at Christmas. It is also known as Siena cake for the city in which it originated.

Panini: Panino is the Italian term for "small sandwich" and panini is the plural form of the word. These sandwiches are typically made using a small loaf of ciabatta bread and grilled. The word "panini" is often used in America as the both the singular and the plural.

Panzanella: A salad with Tuscan origins, panzanella was created by thrifty cooks as a way to use stale bread. Panzanella includes cubed bread, tomatoes, onions and an olive oil vinaigrette dressing.

Pasta e Fagioli: Literally translated as "pasta and beans," this popular hearty Italian soup has many variations but usually features cannellini beans and a small shaped pasta, such as orecchiette, ditali or macaroni.

Pecorino Cheese: Pecorino is an Italian term that refers to cheeses made from sheep's milk. The most well-known pecorino is pecorino Romano, a sharp, tangy hard cheese that can be substituted for Parmesan cheese.

Penne: A common pasta, penne is a short straight tube of pasta that is cut diagonally; it is smooth, unlike its cousin rigatoni, which is ridged.

Peperonata: A mixture of bell peppers, onions, garlic and tomatoes sautéed in olive oil, peperonata is traditionally served at room temperature as a condiment with meat, but can also be served as part of an antipasti selection.

Peperoncini: Small thin hot peppers that are pickled, peperoncini are often used as a garnish or as part of an antipasti selection.

Pesce: Pesce is the Italian term for "fish."

Pesto: A popular uncooked pasta sauce from the Ligurian region, pesto is made from fresh basil leaves, garlic, pine nuts (or walnuts), olive oil and Parmesan cheese. It is traditionally prepared by crushing the ingredients in a mortar with a pestle, but modern cooks favor a food processor.

Piccata: This term is used to describe a preparation method for veal and sometimes chicken or pork. Typically veal piccata is made with thin cutlets that are dredged in seasoned flour and quickly  sautéed in butter or olive oil; the skillet is deglazed with broth or wine and the veal is served with the pan juices and topped with grated lemon peel and chopped parsley.

Pine Nuts: Pine nuts (pinoli) are the seeds of pine cones from a Mediterranean tree. They are high in fat and an important ingredient in pesto.

Pizzaiola: A tomato sauce made from fresh tomatoes, onions, bell peppers and garlic, pizzaiola originated in Naples. It got its name from pizza, because it is made with ingredients often used to top pizza. It is served with pasta and sometimes beef.

Polenta: Made from cornmeal, polenta is prepared by cooking cornmeal in water until a thick, spoonable mixture is formed. It can be served as a side dish and topped with sauce. Polenta can also be cooled in a pan, sliced, then panfried or grilled until crispy.

Pollo: Pollo is the Italian term for a "young chicken," such as a broiler-fryer.

Pomodoro: The Italian term for "tomato," al pomodora means to serve with a tomato sauce.

Porcini: Wild, fresh, brown Italian mushrooms, porcini have an intense earthy flavor. They are usually available only dried in America.

Prosciutto: Prosciutto refers to "Italian ham," which is salt-cured but not smoked. Prosciutto di Parma is considered the highest quality. Where and how the prosciutto is produced is strictly controlled by the Italian government. In the United States it is available sliced and prepackaged.

Provolone: A traditional cheese from the Campania region, the smoky-flavored provolone has a waxy brown rind and a sharp flavor. It is made from cow's milk and aged for two or three months. It is formed into various shapes, but a pear shape is common.

Puttanesca: Puttanesca refers to a spicy pasta sauce made with fresh tomatoes, onions, black olives, capers, garlic, oregano and anchovies.

Radiatore: This Italian term is translated literally as "little radiators" and refers to a distinctively shaped pasta with rippled edges.

Radicchio: A reddish-purple leafy salad ingredient, radicchio has a bitter flavor similar to Belgian endive.

Ragù: Ragù is an Italian term for "meat sauce." It usually refers to Bolognese sauce.

Ricotta: A soft unripened cheese, Italian ricotta cheese is made from whey, a by-product of the cheese-making process. American ricotta is often made from whey and milk.

Rigatoni: Short straight tubes of pasta, rigatoni is often ridged.

Riso: Riso is the Italian term for "rice." Risi e bisi is a popular Venetian rice dish made with fresh peas.

Risotto: Risotto is a classic rice dish from northern Italy. Risotto is made with a special short-grain rice called arborio. The rice is sautéed briefly in butter or olive oil, then hot broth is added in small amounts while the rice mixture is constantly stirred to produce a creamy result. Common additions to risotto are Parmesan cheese, wine and vegetables.

Romano cheese: In Italy, Romano cheese may be made from sheep's, goat's or cow's milk, but the best known is pecorino Romano, which is made from sheep's milk. The Romano cheese produced in the United States is most often a milder version made with cow's milk.

Rotini: A common variety of pasta, rotini is shaped like short springs.

Salame: Italian for "salami," this family of cured sausages is usually made from pork. There are many types; the most common to Americans are the highly seasoned cotto salame with black peppercorns and Genoa salame with white peppercorns.

Salsa: This Italian term means "sauce."

Salumi: A general term, salumi refers to cured meats, such as salame and prosciutto.

Scaloppine: This term refers to a method of preparation in which thin, boneless pieces of meat (usually veal) or poultry are coated lightly with flour then quickly sautéed in butter or olive oil. A scaloppine dish is often served with a simple Marsala wine sauce made from the pan drippings, a lemon-flavored sauce or tomato sauce.

Saltimbocca: A special Roman preparation style in which a veal cutlet is pounded into a thin piece, then topped with prosciutto and chopped sage before sautéing in butter. Pounded boneless chicken breasts can be substituted for veal; sometimes the chicken is rolled before cooking.

Scampi: Scampi is the Italian term for "saltwater prawns," which are the tails of small lobsters. They are similar in appearance to shrimp. In America scampi refers to a broiled or grilled shrimp dish prepared with garlic and butter or olive oil.

Tagliatelle: Tagliatelle is the term used in some regions of Italy to refer to ribbons of fresh pasta that resemble fettuccine.

Tetrazzini: An American term for a dish or casserole of spaghetti, chicken or turkey pieces and Parmesan cheese baked in a sherry cream sauce.

Tiramisù: A well-known rich classic Italian dessert, traditional tiramisù consists of espresso- or wine-soaked ladyfingers or sponge cake layered with mascarpone cheese, shaved chocolate and whipped cream. It is believed to be a creation of a restaurant in Treviso during the 1960s.

Torta: Torta is the Italian term for "cake."

Tortellini: A traditional pasta, tortellini is filled, folded and shaped into a ring.

Vermicelli: This term refers to long thin strands of pasta. Shaped like spaghetti, vermicelli is much thinner.

Zabaglione: A light, thin wine-flavored egg custard, zabaglione is served as a sauce or alone as a dessert.

Antipasti and Soups

page 36

page 34

page 46

Italian dinners begin with an antipasto course, which includes savory bits of cheese, meat, vegetables and olives. Crostini and bruschetta are popular, too. A delicious soup packed with flavor is often served next. You're sure to find an antipasto recipe to get your next dinner party off to a fabulous start or a tasty soup to please your entire family.

Margherita Panini Bites

pictured on page 17

  1 loaf (16 ounces) ciabatta or crusty Italian bread, cut into 16 (½-inch) slices
  8 teaspoons prepared pesto
16 fresh basil leaves
  8 slices (1 ounce each) mozzarella cheese
24 thin slices plum tomatoes (about 2 large tomatoes)
    Olive oil

1. Spread each of 8 slices bread with 1 teaspoon pesto. Top each slice with 2 basil leaves, 1 slice mozzarella cheese and 3 slices tomatoes. Top with remaining slices bread.

2. Brush both sides of sandwiches lightly with olive oil. Grill sandwiches in stovetop grill pan, indoor grill or skillet until lightly browned.

3. Cut each sandwich into 4 pieces. Serve warm.   *Makes 32 panini bites*

Bean and Rice Soup

3 ounces thinly sliced pancetta, chopped (about ½ cup)
1 cup chopped onion
2 quarts (four 10½-ounce cans) beef broth
2 cans (14½ ounces each) CONTADINA® Recipe Ready Diced Tomatoes with
    Roasted Garlic, undrained
1 tablespoon chopped fresh rosemary *or* 1 teaspoon dried rosemary leaves, crushed
1 cup arborio or long-grain white rice, uncooked
¼ teaspoon salt
¼ teaspoon ground black pepper
1 can (15½ ounces) Great Northern white beans, drained
2 tablespoons chopped fresh Italian parsley

1. Sauté pancetta for 1 minute in large saucepan.

2. Add onion; sauté for 2 to 3 minutes or just until pancetta is crisp. Add broth, tomatoes with juice and rosemary. Bring to a boil.

3. Reduce heat to low; simmer, uncovered, for 10 minutes. Add rice, salt and pepper; simmer, covered, for 20 to 25 minutes or until rice is tender.

4. Add beans; simmer for 5 minutes. Sprinkle with parsley just before serving.   *Makes 10 cups*

Note: Substitute 3 bacon slices for 3 ounces pancetta.

Antipasto with Marinated Mushrooms

      Marinated Mushrooms (recipe follows)
  4 teaspoons red wine vinegar
  ½ teaspoon dried basil
  ½ teaspoon dried oregano
      Generous dash black pepper
  ¼ cup extra-virgin olive oil
  4 ounces mozzarella cheese, cut into ½-inch cubes
  4 ounces prosciutto or cooked ham, thinly sliced
  4 ounces provolone cheese, cut into 2-inch sticks
  1 jar (10 ounces) peperoncini peppers, drained
  8 ounces hard salami, thinly sliced
  2 jars (6 ounces each) marinated artichoke hearts, drained
  1 can (6 ounces) pitted ripe olives, drained

1. Prepare Marinated Mushrooms; set aside. Combine vinegar, basil, oregano and black pepper in small bowl. Add oil; whisk until well blended. Add mozzarella cubes; stir to coat. Marinate, covered, in refrigerator at least 2 hours.

2. Drain mozzarella, reserving marinade. Wrap half of prosciutto slices around provolone sticks; roll up remaining slices. Arrange mozzarella cubes, prosciutto-wrapped provolone, prosciutto rolls, Marinated Mushrooms, peperoncini, salami, artichoke hearts and olives on large platter. Drizzle reserved marinade over peperoncini, artichoke hearts and olives.   *Makes 6 to 8 servings*

Marinated Mushrooms

  3 tablespoons lemon juice
  2 tablespoons chopped fresh Italian parsley
  1 clove garlic, crushed
  ½ teaspoon salt
  ¼ teaspoon dried tarragon
  ⅛ teaspoon black pepper
  ½ cup extra-virgin olive oil
  ½ pound small or medium fresh mushrooms, stems removed

1. Combine lemon juice, parsley, garlic, salt, tarragon and pepper in medium bowl. Add oil; whisk until well blended. Add mushrooms; stir to coat. Marinate, covered, in refrigerator 4 hours or overnight, stirring occasionally.

2. Drain mushrooms; refrigerate marinade for another use.

Pepperoni-Oregano Focaccia

    1 tablespoon cornmeal
    1 package (10 ounces) refrigerated pizza crust dough
    ½ cup finely chopped pepperoni (3 to 3½ ounces)
  1½ teaspoons finely chopped fresh oregano *or* ½ teaspoon dried oregano
    2 teaspoons extra-virgin olive oil

1. Preheat oven to 425°F. Spray baking sheet with nonstick cooking spray; sprinkle with cornmeal. Set aside.

2. Unroll dough onto lightly floured surface. Pat dough into 12×9-inch rectangle. Sprinkle half of pepperoni and half of oregano over one side of dough. Fold over dough, making 12×4½-inch rectangle.

3. Roll dough into 12×9-inch rectangle. Place on prepared baking sheet. Prick dough with fork at 2-inch intervals about 30 times. Brush with oil; sprinkle with remaining pepperoni and oregano.

4. Bake 12 to 15 minutes or until golden brown. (Prick dough several more times during baking if dough puffs up.) Cut into strips. *Makes 12 servings*

Bruschetta

    2 Italian rolls (each 5 inches long)
    1 can (14½ ounces) CONTADINA® Recipe Ready Diced Tomatoes, drained
    2 tablespoons chopped fresh basil
    1 tablespoon finely chopped onion
    1 tablespoon olive oil
    1 small clove garlic, crushed
    ¼ teaspoon dried oregano leaves, crushed
    ¼ teaspoon salt
    ⅛ teaspoon ground black pepper

1. Slice rolls in half lengthwise; toast.

2. Combine tomatoes, basil, onion, olive oil, garlic, oregano, salt and pepper in small bowl. Spoon mixture onto toasted rolls.

3. Broil 5 inches from heat source until hot, about 2 minutes. *Makes 8 appetizer servings*

Prep Time: 10 minutes • **Cook Time:** 2 minutes

Pepperoni-Oregano Focaccia

Italian Beef and Barley Soup

1 boneless beef top sirloin (about 1½ pounds)
1 tablespoon vegetable oil
4 medium carrots or parsnips, cut into ¼-inch slices
1 cup chopped onion
1 teaspoon dried thyme
½ teaspoon dried rosemary
¼ teaspoon black pepper
⅓ cup pearl barley
2 cans (14½ ounces each) beef broth
1 can (14½ ounces) diced tomatoes with Italian seasoning, undrained

Slow Cooker Directions

1. Cut beef into 1-inch pieces. Heat oil over medium-high heat in large skillet. Brown beef on all sides; set aside.

2. Place carrots and onion in slow cooker; sprinkle with thyme, rosemary and pepper. Top with barley and beef. Pour broth and tomatoes with juice over meat.

3. Cover; cook on LOW 8 to 10 hours or until beef is tender.   *Makes 6 servings*

Tip: Choose pearl barley rather than quick-cooking barley because it will stand up to long cooking.

Prep Time: 20 minutes • **Cook Time:** 8 to 10 hours

Italian Beef and Barley Soup

Eggplant Rolls

1 large eggplant (about 1¼ pounds)
3 tablespoons olive oil
   Salt and black pepper
1 cup whole milk ricotta cheese
½ cup grated Asiago cheese
¼ cup julienned or chopped sun-dried tomatoes packed in oil
¼ cup chopped fresh basil or Italian parsley
⅛ teaspoon red pepper flakes
   Fresh basil or thyme sprigs (optional)

1. Preheat broiler. Trim off stem end from eggplant; peel eggplant, if desired. Cut eggplant lengthwise into 6 long, thin slices about ¼ inch thick. Brush both sides of eggplant slices with oil; sprinkle with salt and pepper to taste. Place on rack of broiler pan.

2. Broil eggplant 4 inches from heat source 4 to 5 minutes per side or until golden brown and slightly softened. Let eggplant cool to room temperature.

3. Combine ricotta cheese, Asiago cheese, sun-dried tomatoes, basil and red pepper flakes in small bowl; mix well. Spread mixture evenly over cooled eggplant slices. Roll up and cut each roll in half diagonally. Arrange seam side down on serving platter; garnish with basil. Serve warm or at room temperature.   *Makes 6 appetizer servings*

BelGioioso® Gorgonzola Spread

2 cups BELGIOIOSO® Mascarpone
½ cup BELGIOIOSO® Gorgonzola
2 tablespoons chopped fresh basil
½ cup chopped walnuts
   Sliced apples and pears

In small bowl, combine BelGioioso Mascarpone, BelGioioso Gorgonzola and basil. Mix to blend well. Transfer mixture to serving bowl; cover and refrigerate 2 hours. Before serving, sprinkle with walnuts and arrange sliced apples and pears around bowl.   *Makes 8 servings*

Tip: This spread can also be served with fresh vegetables, crackers, Melba toast or bread.

Tomato and Caper Crostini

   1 ciabatta sandwich roll or French roll, cut into 8 slices
   2 plum tomatoes, finely chopped (about 4 ounces)
1½ tablespoons capers
1½ teaspoons dried basil
   1 teaspoon extra-virgin olive oil
   1 ounce crumbled feta cheese with sun-dried tomatoes and basil, or any variety

1. Preheat oven to 350°F.

2. Place bread slices on ungreased baking sheet in single layer. Bake 15 minutes or just until golden brown. Cool completely.

3. Meanwhile, combine tomatoes, capers, basil and oil in small bowl; mix well.

4. Just before serving, spoon tomato mixture on each bread slice; sprinkle with cheese.

Makes 2 servings

Pappa al Pomodoro alla Papa Newman (Bread and Tomato Soup)

  ¾ cup olive oil plus extra for drizzling on soup, divided
   3 large cloves garlic, smashed
   1 teaspoon dried sage
 12 ounces stale Italian or French bread, thinly sliced, crusts removed (about 30 slices), divided
   1 jar NEWMAN'S OWN® Bombolina Sauce (about 3 cups)
   4 cups chicken broth
  ½ teaspoon hot red pepper flakes
  ½ teaspoon freshly ground black pepper
    Freshly grated Parmesan cheese

1. In large skillet, heat ¼ cup oil over medium heat. Add garlic and sage and cook, stirring frequently, 1 to 2 minutes. Remove garlic from oil. Add ⅓ of bread slices and cook, turning once, until golden brown on both sides, 2 to 3 minutes per side. Remove from heat; repeat with remaining oil and bread.

2. In large heavy saucepan, heat Newman's Own® Bombolina Sauce and chicken broth over medium-high heat to boiling. Reduce heat to low. Add red pepper flakes, black pepper and bread; simmer, covered, 30 minutes. Remove from heat and let stand 30 minutes to 1 hour. Ladle into soup bowls. Drizzle lightly with olive oil and sprinkle with Parmesan cheese. *Makes 6 to 8 servings*

Bean & Pasta Soup

d elbow macaroni
live oil
, chopped
inced

2 cans (14½ ounces each) reduced-sodium chicken broth
1 jar (26 ounces) marinara sauce
1 can (15 ounces) cannellini or Great Northern beans, rinsed and drained
2 teaspoons balsamic vinegar
1 pound fresh spinach, chopped
½ cup grated Parmesan cheese

1. Cook macaroni according to package directions; drain.

2. Meanwhile, heat oil in Dutch oven or large saucepan over medium heat. Add onion and garlic; cook and stir 5 minutes or until onion is tender.

3. Stir in water, broth, marinara sauce and beans; bring to a boil. Reduce heat to low; cook, uncovered, 10 minutes, stirring occasionally. Stir in vinegar, then spinach and cooked pasta; cook 5 minutes. Sprinkle with cheese before serving.   *Makes 10 to 12 servings*

Pesto-Parmesan Twists

1 loaf frozen bread dough, thawed
¼ cup prepared pesto sauce
⅔ cup grated Parmesan cheese, divided
1 tablespoon olive oil

1. Line baking sheets with parchment paper. Roll out dough to 20×10-inch rectangle on lightly floured surface.

2. Spread pesto evenly over half of dough; sprinkle with ⅓ cup cheese. Fold remaining half of dough over filling, forming 10-inch square. Roll square into 12×10-inch rectangle. Cut into 12 (1-inch) strips with sharp knife. Cut strips in half crosswise to form 24 strips total.

3. Twist each strip several times; place on prepared baking sheets. Cover with towel or plastic wrap; let rise in warm, draft-free place 20 minutes.

4. Preheat oven to 350°F. Brush breadsticks with oil; sprinkle with remaining ⅓ cup cheese. Bake 16 to 18 minutes or until golden brown.   *Makes 24 breadsticks*

Hearty Bean & Pasta Soup

Focaccia

1 cup water
1 tablespoon olive oil, plus additional for brushing
1 teaspoon salt
1 tablespoon sugar
3 cups bread flour
2¼ teaspoons (1 packet) RED STAR® Active Dry Yeast or QUICK•RISE™ Yeast or
    Bread Machine Yeast
  Suggested toppings: sun-dried tomatoes, roasted bell pepper slices, sautéed onion rings,
    fresh and dried herbs in any combination, grated hard cheese

Bread Machine Method
Place room temperature ingredients except toppings in pan in order listed. Select dough cycle.
Check dough consistency after 5 minutes of kneading, making adjustments if necessary.

Hand-Held Mixer Method
Combine yeast, 1 cup flour, sugar and salt. Combine water and 1 tablespoon oil; heat mixture to
120° to 130°F. Combine dry and liquid mixtures in mixing bowl on low speed. Beat 2 to 3 minutes
on medium speed. By hand, stir in enough remaining flour to make a firm dough. Knead on
floured surface 5 to 7 minutes or until smooth and elastic. Add additional flour, if necessary.

Stand Mixer Method
Combine yeast, 1 cup flour, sugar and salt. Combine water and 1 tablespoon oil; heat mixture to
120° to 130°F. Combine dry and liquid mixtures in mixing bowl with paddle or beaters for
4 minutes on medium speed. Gradually add remaining flour and knead with dough hook 5 to
7 minutes or until smooth and elastic. Add additional flour, if necessary.

Rising, Shaping and Baking
Place dough in lightly oiled bowl and turn to grease top. Cover; let rise until dough tests ripe.* Turn
dough onto lightly floured surface; punch down to remove air bubbles. On lightly floured surface,
shape dough into a ball. Place on greased baking sheet. Flatten to 14-inch circle. With knife, cut
circle in dough about 1 inch from edge, cutting almost through to baking sheet. Pierce center with
fork. Cover; let rise about 15 minutes. Brush with oil and sprinkle with desired toppings. Bake in
preheated 375°F oven 25 to 30 minutes or until golden brown. Remove from baking sheet to cool.
Serve warm or at room temperature.   *Makes 1 (14-inch) loaf*

*Place two fingers into the risen dough up to the second knuckle, then remove. If the indentations remain the
dough is ripe and ready to punch down.*

Note: When flattening dough into circle, if the dough does not stretch easily, let it rest a couple of
minutes; then press it out. Repeat if necessary.

Onion and Pepper Calzones

     1 teaspoon olive oil
     ½ cup chopped onion
     ½ cup chopped green bell pepper
     ¼ teaspoon salt
     ⅛ teaspoon dried basil
     ⅛ teaspoon dried oregano
     ⅛ teaspoon black pepper
     1 can (12 ounces) country biscuits (10 biscuits)
     ¼ cup (1 ounce) shredded mozzarella cheese
     ½ cup prepared pasta or pizza sauce
     2 tablespoons grated Parmesan cheese

1. Preheat oven to 400°F. Heat oil in medium nonstick skillet over medium heat. Add onion and bell pepper; cook 5 minutes or until tender, stirring occasionally. Remove from heat. Add salt, basil, oregano and black pepper; stir to combine. Remove from heat; cool slightly.

2. Meanwhile, flatten biscuits on cutting board into 3½-inch circles about ⅛ inch thick using palm of hand.

3. Stir mozzarella cheese into onion mixture. Spoon 1 teaspoon onion mixture onto each biscuit. Fold biscuits in half, covering filling. Press edges with tines of fork to seal; transfer to baking sheet.

4. Bake 10 to 12 minutes or until golden brown. Meanwhile, place pasta sauce in small microwavable bowl. Cover with vented plastic wrap. Microwave on HIGH 3 minutes or until hot.

5. Spoon pasta sauce and Parmesan cheese evenly over each calzone. Serve immediately.

Makes 10 calzones

Prep and Cook Time: 25 minutes

First brought to large cities like New York and Chicago by Italian immigrants in the late 1800s, pizza and calzones didn't become popular until American soldiers returning from Italy after World War II raved about these delicious treats from Naples.

Onion and Pepper Calzones

Asparagus & Prosciutto Antipasto

  12 fresh asparagus spears (about 8 ounces)
  2 ounces cream cheese, softened
  ¼ cup crumbled blue cheese or goat cheese
  ¼ teaspoon black pepper
  1 package (3 to 4 ounces) thinly sliced prosciutto

1. Trim asparagus spears. Simmer asparagus in salted water in large skillet 4 to 5 minutes or until crisp-tender. (Cooking time will vary depending on thickness of asparagus.) Drain and immediately immerse in cold water to stop cooking.

2. Meanwhile, combine cream cheese, blue cheese and pepper in small bowl; mix well. Cut prosciutto slices in half crosswise to form 12 pieces. Spread cream cheese mixture evenly over one side of each prosciutto slice.

3. Drain asparagus; pat dry with paper towels. Wrap each asparagus spear with one piece prosciutto. Serve at room temperature or slightly chilled.   *Makes 4 servings*

Pasta e Fagioli

pictured on page 16

  2 tablespoons olive oil
  1 cup chopped onion
  3 cloves garlic, minced
  2 cans (14½ ounces each) Italian-style stewed tomatoes, undrained
  3 cups reduced-sodium chicken broth
  1 can (about 15 ounces) cannellini beans,* undrained
  ¼ cup chopped fresh Italian parsley
  1 teaspoon dried basil
  ¼ teaspoon black pepper
  4 ounces uncooked small shell pasta

One can (about 15 ounces) Great Northern beans, undrained, can be substituted for cannellini beans.

1. Heat oil in 4-quart Dutch oven over medium heat. Add onion and garlic; cook and stir 5 minutes or until onion is tender.

2. Add tomatoes with juice, broth, beans with liquid, parsley, basil and pepper to Dutch oven; bring to a boil over high heat, stirring occasionally. Reduce heat to low. Simmer, covered, 10 minutes.

3. Add pasta to Dutch oven. Simmer, covered, 10 to 12 minutes or until pasta is just tender. Serve immediately.   *Makes 8 servings*

Asparagus & Prosciutto Antipasto

Tuscan Chicken with White Beans

1 large fennel bulb (about ¾ pound)
1 teaspoon olive oil
1 teaspoon dried rosemary
½ teaspoon black pepper
½ pound boneless skinless chicken thighs, cut into ¾-inch pieces
1 can (14½ ounces) stewed tomatoes, undrained
1 can (about 14 ounces) reduced-sodium chicken broth
1 can (15 ounces) cannellini beans, rinsed and drained
Hot pepper sauce (optional)

1. Cut off feathery fennel tops. Chop enough to measure ¼ cup; reserve. Chop bulb into ½-inch pieces. Heat oil in large saucepan over medium heat. Add chopped fennel bulb; cook 5 minutes, stirring occasionally.

2. Sprinkle rosemary and pepper over chicken; add to saucepan. Cook and stir 2 minutes. Add tomatoes with juice and broth; bring to a boil. Cover; simmer 10 minutes. Stir in beans; simmer, uncovered, 15 minutes or until chicken is cooked through and sauce thickens. Season to taste with hot pepper sauce. Sprinkle with reserved fennel tops before serving.   *Makes 4 servings*

Hearty Tortellini Soup

pictured on page 16

1 small red onion, chopped
2 medium carrots, chopped
2 ribs celery, thinly sliced
1 small zucchini, chopped
2 plum tomatoes, chopped
2 cloves garlic, minced
2 cans (14½ ounces each) chicken broth
1 can (15 to 19 ounces) red kidney beans, rinsed and drained
2 tablespoons *French's*® Worcestershire Sauce
1 package (9 ounces) refrigerated tortellini pasta

1. Heat *2 tablespoons oil* in 6-quart saucepot or Dutch oven over medium-high heat. Add vegetables, tomatoes and garlic. Cook and stir 5 minutes or until vegetables are crisp-tender.

2. Add broth, *½ cup water,* beans and Worcestershire. Heat to boiling. Stir in pasta. Return to boiling. Cook 5 minutes or until pasta is tender, stirring occasionally. Serve with crusty bread and grated Parmesan cheese, if desired.   *Makes 4 servings*

Prep Time: 15 minutes • **Cook Time:** 10 minutes

Tuscan Chicken with White Beans

Italian-Style Meatball Soup

½ **pound ground beef**
¼ **pound bulk mild Italian sausage**
 1 **large onion, finely chopped, divided**
⅓ **cup dry bread crumbs**
 1 **egg**
½ **teaspoon salt**
 4 **cups beef broth**
 2 **cups water**
 1 **can (8 ounces) stewed tomatoes**
 1 **can (8 ounces) pizza sauce**
 2 **cups sliced cabbage**
 1 **can (15½ ounces) kidney beans, drained**
 2 **medium carrots, sliced**
½ **cup frozen Italian green beans**

1. Combine beef, sausage, 2 tablespoons onion, bread crumbs, egg and salt in large bowl; mix until well blended. Shape into 32 (1-inch) meatballs.

2. Brown half the meatballs in large skillet over medium heat, turning frequently and shaking skillet to keep meatballs round. Remove from skillet and drain on paper towels. Repeat with remaining meatballs.

3. Bring broth, water, tomatoes and pizza sauce to a boil in Dutch oven over high heat. Add meatballs, remaining onion, cabbage, kidney beans and carrots. Bring to a boil. Reduce heat; simmer, uncovered, 20 minutes. Add green beans; return to a boil. Reduce heat and simmer, uncovered, 10 minutes.

Makes 8 servings

Italian-Style Meatball Soup

Mediterranean Frittata

¼ cup extra-virgin olive oil
5 small onions, thinly sliced
1 can (about 14 ounces) whole peeled tomatoes, drained and chopped
¼ pound prosciutto, chopped
¼ cup grated Parmesan cheese
2 tablespoons chopped fresh parsley
½ teaspoon dried marjoram
¼ teaspoon salt
¼ teaspoon dried basil
⅛ teaspoon black pepper
6 eggs
2 tablespoons butter or margarine
Italian parsley leaves

1. Heat oil in medium skillet over medium-high heat. Add onions; cook and stir 6 to 8 minutes until soft and golden. Add tomatoes; cook over medium heat 5 minutes. Remove tomatoes and onions to large bowl with slotted spoon; discard drippings. Cool tomato mixture to room temperature.

2. Stir prosciutto, cheese, parsley, marjoram, salt, basil and pepper into cooled tomato mixture. Whisk eggs in small bowl; stir into prosciutto mixture.

3. Preheat broiler. Heat butter in large broilerproof skillet over medium heat until melted and bubbly; reduce heat to low. Add egg mixture to skillet, spreading evenly. Cook over low heat 8 to 10 minutes until all but top ¼ inch of egg mixture is set; shake pan gently to test. *Do not stir.*

4. Place pan under broiler about 4 inches from heat. Broil 1 to 2 minutes until top of egg mixture is set. (Do not brown or frittata will be dry.) Cut into wedges. Serve hot or at room temperature. Garnish with parsley.

Makes 6 to 8 appetizer servings

Prosciutto is Italian salt-cured ham. Unlike most American ham, it is not smoked. Look for it at the deli counter or with packaged deli meats. You may substitute boiled ham or smoked ham but the flavor of the frittata will be different.

Mediterranean Frittata

Sicilian Caponata

    5 tablespoons olive or vegetable oil, divided
    8 cups (1½ pounds) cubed unpeeled eggplant
  2½ cups onion slices
    1 cup chopped celery
    1 can (14½ ounces) CONTADINA® Recipe Ready Diced Tomatoes with
        Roasted Garlic, undrained
  ⅓ cup chopped pitted ripe olives, drained
  ¼ cup balsamic or red wine vinegar
    2 tablespoons capers
    2 teaspoons granulated sugar
  ½ teaspoon salt
    Dash of ground black pepper

1. Heat 3 tablespoons oil in large skillet. Add eggplant; sauté 6 minutes. Remove eggplant from skillet.

2. Heat remaining oil in same skillet. Add onions and celery; sauté 5 minutes or until vegetables are tender.

3. Stir in undrained tomatoes and eggplant; cover. Simmer 15 minutes or until eggplant is tender.

4. Stir in olives, vinegar, capers, sugar, salt and pepper; simmer, uncovered, 5 minutes, stirring occasionally. Serve with toasted bread slices, if desired.   *Makes 4½ cups*

Carpaccio di Zucchini

  12 ounces zucchini, shredded
  ½ cup sliced almonds, toasted
    1 tablespoon Italian dressing
    4 French rolls, cut in half lengthwise
    1 tablespoon olive oil
    3 tablespoons grated Parmesan cheese

1. Preheat broiler. Place zucchini in medium bowl. Add almonds and dressing; mix well. Set aside.

2. Place roll halves on baking sheet; brush with olive oil. Sprinkle with cheese. Broil 3 inches from heat 2 to 3 minutes or until edges of bread and cheese are browned.

3. Spread zucchini mixture evenly onto each roll half. Serve immediately.   *Makes 4 servings*

Serving Suggestion: Serve with spaghetti and tomato sauce.

Prep and Cook Time: 28 minutes

Sicilian Caponata

Primavera Tortellini en Brodo

2 cans (about 14 ounces each) reduced-sodium chicken broth
1 package (9 ounces) refrigerated fresh tortellini (cheese, chicken or sausage)
2 cups frozen mixed vegetables, such as broccoli, green beans, onions and red bell peppers
1 teaspoon dried basil
Dash hot pepper sauce
1 tablespoon water
2 teaspoons cornstarch
¼ cup grated Romano or Parmesan cheese

1. Pour broth into large deep skillet; cover and bring to a boil over high heat. Add tortellini; reduce heat to medium-high. Cook, uncovered, until pasta is tender, stirring occasionally.

2. Transfer tortellini to medium bowl with slotted spoon; keep warm.

3. Add vegetables, basil and hot pepper sauce to broth; bring to a boil. Reduce heat; simmer about 3 minutes or until vegetables are crisp-tender.

4. Blend water and cornstarch in small cup until smooth. Stir into broth mixture. Cook about 2 minutes or until liquid thickens slightly, stirring frequently. Return tortellini to skillet; heat through. Sprinkle with cheese before serving.   *Makes 2 servings*

Serving Suggestion: Serve with salad and crusty Italian bread.

Prep and Cook Time: 20 minutes

Onion & White Bean Spread

1 can (about 15 ounces) cannellini or Great Northern beans, rinsed and drained
2 cloves garlic, minced
¼ cup minced green onion
¼ cup grated Parmesan cheese
¼ cup extra-virgin olive oil, plus more for serving
1 tablespoon finely chopped fresh rosemary
French bread slices

1. Combine all ingredients except bread slices in food processor. Process 30 to 40 seconds or until mixture is almost smooth.

2. Spoon mixture into serving bowl. Drizzle top with additional olive oil; serve with French bread slices.   *Makes 1¼ cups spread*

Tip: For a more rustic spread, place all ingredients in a medium bowl and use a potato masher to mash beans and combine ingredients.

Primavera Tortellini en Brodo

Italian Bean and Tomato Soup

    1 can (about 16 ounces) kidney beans, undrained
    1 can (about 16 ounces) white cannellini beans
    1 can (about 15 ounces) Italian stewed tomatoes
    1 can (about 14 ounces) ready-to-serve chicken broth
    ½ cup small pasta shells (uncooked)

In a medium saucepan, combine kidney and cannellini beans, tomatoes, chicken broth and pasta shells. Bring to a boil. Reduce heat and simmer, covered, until pasta is cooked, about 10 minutes. Serve with grated Parmesan cheese and garnish with parsley, if desired. Try this with a few fresh mushrooms. *Makes about 6½ cups*

Favorite recipe from **Mushroom Council**

Mama Mia Minestrone Magnifico

    2 tablespoons extra-virgin olive oil
    8 ounces crimini mushrooms, cut into ½-inch pieces (3 cups)
    1 yellow summer squash (6 ounces), cut into ½-inch cubes (1¼ cups)
    ½ small eggplant, cut into ½-inch cubes (1 cup)
    4 ounces green beans, cut diagonally into ½-inch pieces (1 cup)
    6 cups water
    1 (26-ounce) jar NEWMAN'S OWN® Roasted Garlic and Peppers Sauce
    1 cup Burgundy wine
    1 cup uncooked orzo pasta
    1 (15½- to 19-ounce) can white kidney beans (cannellini), drained
    4 medium tomatoes (16 ounces), chopped (2 cups)
    4 fresh basil leaves, chopped
    1 tablespoon chopped fresh Italian parsley
    ¾ cup freshly grated Parmesan cheese
    ½ cup pine nuts, toasted

In 12-inch nonstick skillet, heat oil; sauté mushrooms, squash, eggplant and green beans over medium-high heat 10 minutes, stirring constantly, until golden and tender.

Combine water, pasta sauce and wine in 6-quart saucepot and bring to a boil. Add orzo and simmer 10 minutes, stirring occasionally.

Add sautéed vegetables, white beans, chopped tomatoes, basil and parsley; simmer 5 minutes, stirring occasionally.

Serve with Parmesan cheese and pine nuts to sprinkle on top. *Makes 8 servings*

Italian Bean and Tomato Soup

Pasta and Rice

page 70

page 54

page 62

What is more Italian than pasta? There's a pasta for every dish—from long thin spaghetti and flat lasagna noodles to ravioli pockets and an endless variety of shapes. While pasta may be king, Italians have a way with rice, too. Rice is a star that truly shines in creamy Italian risottos. Make one of these pasta or rice recipes the center of attraction at dinner tonight.

Manicotti

1 container (16 ounces) ricotta cheese
2 cups (8 ounces) shredded mozzarella cheese
½ cup cottage cheese
2 eggs, beaten
2 tablespoons grated Parmesan cheese
½ teaspoon minced garlic
   Salt and black pepper
1 package (about 8 ounces) uncooked manicotti shells
1 pound ground beef
1 jar (26 ounces) pasta sauce
2 cups water

1. Combine ricotta cheese, mozzarella cheese, cottage cheese, eggs, Parmesan cheese and garlic in large bowl; mix well. Season with salt and pepper.

2. Stuff mixture into manicotti shells using small spoon. Place filled shells in 13×9-inch baking dish. Preheat oven to 375°F.

3. Brown ground beef in large skillet over medium-high heat, stirring to separate meat. Drain fat. Stir in pasta sauce and water (mixture will be thin). Pour sauce over filled manicotti shells.

4. Cover with foil; bake 1 hour or until sauce has thickened and shells are tender.   *Makes 6 servings*

Pasta with Four Cheeses

¾ cup uncooked ziti or rigatoni
3 tablespoons butter, divided
½ cup grated CUCINA CLASSICA ITALIANA® Parmesan cheese, divided
¼ teaspoon ground nutmeg, divided
¼ cup GALBANI® Mascarpone
¾ cup (about 3½ ounces) shredded mozzarella cheese
¾ cup (about 3½ ounces) shredded BEL PAESE® semi-soft cheese

Preheat oven to 350°F. Lightly grease 1-quart casserole. Set aside.

In large saucepan of boiling water, cook pasta until tender but still firm. Drain in colander. Place in large mixing bowl. Stir in 1½ tablespoons butter, ¼ cup Parmesan cheese and ⅛ teaspoon nutmeg.

Spread one fourth of pasta mixture into prepared casserole. Spoon Mascarpone onto pasta. Layer with one fourth of pasta. Top with mozzarella. Add third layer of pasta. Sprinkle with Bel Paese® cheese. Top with remaining pasta. Dot with remaining 1½ tablespoons butter. Sprinkle with remaining ¼ cup Parmesan cheese and ⅛ teaspoon nutmeg. Bake until golden brown, about 20 minutes.   *Makes 4 servings*

Manicotti

Homemade Spinach Ravioli

  1 box (10 ounces) frozen chopped spinach
  1 cup ricotta cheese
  ½ cup grated Romano or Parmesan cheese
  1 egg
  1 tablespoon minced fresh basil
  ½ teaspoon salt
  ½ teaspoon black pepper
  ¼ teaspoon ground nutmeg
 36 wonton wrappers
  1 jar (about 26 ounces) marinara or other pasta sauce
    Fresh spinach and basil leaves (optional)

1. For filling, cook spinach according to package directions. Drain in colander; squeeze out as much liquid as possible. Chop spinach very finely. Place in medium bowl; mix in cheeses, egg, basil, salt, pepper and nutmeg. (May be prepared up to 1 day in advance.)

2. Place 1 or 2 wonton wrappers on lightly floured surface, keeping remaining wrappers covered. Place 1 heaping teaspoon of filling in center of each wrapper. To seal ravioli, moisten edges around filling and place another wrapper on top; press edges gently around filling to remove air bubbles and seal. (If using square wrappers, cut with 1½-inch round or scalloped cookie cutter to make circle, if desired.) Set finished ravioli aside; repeat until all wonton wrappers are used. Leftover filling may be frozen for later use.

3. To cook ravioli, bring large saucepan of salted water to a boil. Meanwhile, heat marinara sauce in medium saucepan over low heat. Add half of ravioli to boiling water; reduce heat to medium-high. Stir gently and cook until ravioli rise to top (about 3 minutes). Remove ravioli with slotted spoon and keep warm. Repeat with remaining ravioli. Serve with marinara sauce; garnish with fresh spinach and basil leaves.

Makes 18 ravioli (about 4 servings)

Wonton wrappers to make ravioli? Why not? Wonton wrappers are made from flour and eggs while pasta is usually made from flour and water (although sometimes eggs are used too). Wonton wrappers are the perfect size to make square or round ravioli and they are readily available in most large supermarkets. Frozen wonton wrappers should be thawed before using them.

Classic Fettuccine Alfredo

12 ounces uncooked fettuccine pasta
⅔ cup whipping cream
6 tablespoons unsalted butter
½ teaspoon salt
    Generous dash white pepper
    Generous dash ground nutmeg
1 cup grated Parmesan cheese
2 tablespoons chopped fresh parsley

1. Cook pasta according to package directions; drain well and return to pan.

2. Heat cream and butter in large heavy skillet over medium-low heat until butter melts and mixture bubbles. Cook and stir 2 minutes more. Stir in salt, pepper and nutmeg. Remove from heat. Gradually stir in cheese until well blended and smooth. Return briefly to heat to completely blend cheese if necessary. (Do not let sauce bubble or cheese will become lumpy and tough.)

3. Pour sauce over pasta. Toss with 2 forks over low heat 2 to 3 minutes until sauce is thickened and pasta is evenly coated. Sprinkle with chopped parsley. Serve immediately.   *Makes 4 servings*

Baked Gnocchi

1 package (about 17 ounces) gnocchi (frozen or vacuum-packed)
⅓ cup olive oil
3 large cloves garlic, minced
1 package (10 ounces) frozen spinach, thawed and squeezed dry
1 can (about 14 ounces) diced tomatoes
1 teaspoon Italian seasoning
    Salt and black pepper
½ cup grated Parmesan cheese
½ cup (2 ounces) shredded mozzarella cheese

1. Bring large saucepan of water to a boil; cook gnocchi according to package directions. Drain and set aside. Butter large casserole or gratin dish. Preheat oven to 350°F.

2. Heat oil in large skillet or Dutch oven over medium heat. Add garlic; cook and stir 30 seconds. Add spinach; cook and stir until spinach wilts (1 to 2 minutes). Add tomatoes and Italian seasoning. Season with salt and pepper; cook and stir about 5 minutes. Add gnocchi to skillet; stir gently.

3. Pour gnocchi mixture into prepared dish. Sprinkle with cheeses. Bake 20 to 30 minutes or until casserole is bubbly and cheese is melted.   *Makes 4 servings*

Pesto Lasagna Rolls

  2 cups fresh basil leaves
  2 cloves garlic
  ¾ cup (3 ounces) SARGENTO® Fancy Parmesan Shredded Cheese, divided
  ¾ cup olive oil
  2 cups (15 ounces) SARGENTO® Whole Milk Ricotta Cheese*
  1 cup (4 ounces) SARGENTO® Reduced Fat Mozzarella Shredded Cheese
  1 egg, beaten
  1 cup diced zucchini
16 lasagna noodles, cooked, drained and cooled

*SARGENTO® Part-Skim Ricotta, Light Ricotta or Fat Free Ricotta can also be used.

Prepare pesto sauce in covered blender or food processor by processing basil with garlic until chopped. Add ½ cup Parmesan cheese; process until well mixed. With machine running, slowly add oil and continue processing until smooth. Set aside. In medium bowl, combine Ricotta and Mozzarella cheeses, remaining ¼ cup Parmesan cheese and egg; blend well. Fold in zucchini. Spread 2 heaping tablespoons cheese mixture on each lasagna noodle. Roll up each noodle individually and stand vertically in greased 11×7-inch baking dish. Pour pesto sauce over lasagna rolls; cover and bake at 350°F 40 minutes or until bubbly and heated through.   *Makes 8 servings*

Classic Pasta Sauce

  1 pound mild Italian sausage with fennel
  ½ cup chopped onion
  2 cloves garlic, minced
  1 can (28 ounces) tomato sauce
  1 can (28 ounces) crushed tomatoes
  ¼ cup red wine (optional)
  1 tablespoon chopped peperoncini
  1 teaspoon dried oregano
  ½ teaspoon dried basil
    Hot cooked pasta
    Grated Parmesan cheese

1. Remove sausage from casings. Cook sausage, onion and garlic in large saucepan over medium-high heat until sausage is no longer pink, stirring to separate meat.

2. Add tomato sauce, crushed tomatoes, wine, if desired, peperoncini, oregano and basil. Simmer over low heat about 30 minutes to blend flavors. Serve over pasta; sprinkle with Parmesan cheese.
          Makes about 7 cups sauce

Pesto Lasagna Rolls

Eggplant & Shrimp over Fusilli

  2 tablespoons olive oil, divided
  1 large eggplant (about 1½ pounds), peeled and cut into 1-inch cubes (about 6 cups)
  ⅔ cup water, divided
  1 medium onion, chopped
  2 cloves garlic, finely chopped
  ¾ teaspoon salt
  ¼ teaspoon ground black pepper
  1 jar (26 ounces) RAGÚ® Light Pasta Sauce
  8 ounces uncooked shrimp, peeled and deveined
  1 box (16 ounces) fusilli pasta or spaghetti, cooked and drained
  1 cup crumbled feta cheese (optional)

In 12-inch nonstick skillet, heat 1 tablespoon olive oil over medium heat. Cook eggplant with ⅓ cup water, covered, stirring occasionally, 15 minutes or until eggplant is tender. Remove eggplant and set aside.

In same skillet, heat remaining 1 tablespoon olive oil over medium heat and cook onion, garlic, salt and pepper 2 minutes or until onion is tender. Stir in Ragú Light Pasta Sauce, remaining ⅓ cup water and eggplant. Reduce heat to low and simmer, covered, stirring occasionally, 6 minutes. Stir in shrimp and simmer, stirring occasionally, 4 minutes or until shrimp turn pink. Serve over hot pasta and garnish with crumbled feta cheese, if desired.   *Makes 6 servings*

Pasta with BelGioioso® Gorgonzola Sauce

  1½ cups whipping cream
  1½ cups (12 ounces) creamy BELGIOIOSO® Gorgonzola Cheese
  1 pound fettuccine, cooked and drained
    Fresh grated BELGIOIOSO® Parmesan Cheese
    Fresh cracked black pepper
    Chopped fresh basil

In medium saucepan, bring cream to a boil over medium heat. Simmer about 5 minutes. Reduce heat to low and stir in BelGioioso Gorgonzola Cheese until melted.

Place cooked pasta into large warm bowl; pour sauce over and toss. Sprinkle with BelGioioso Parmesan Cheese, pepper and basil.   *Makes 6 servings*

Olive Lover's Pasta

1 jar (26 ounces) RAGÚ® ROBUSTO!® Pasta Sauce
1 package (12 ounces) tri-color pasta twists, cooked and drained
1 cup sliced assorted pitted olives
2 tablespoons grated Parmesan cheese

In 2-quart saucepan, heat Pasta Sauce over medium-low heat.

To serve, toss hot pasta with Sauce and olives, then sprinkle with cheese. *Makes 6 servings*

Prep Time: 20 minutes • Cook Time: 5 minutes

Tuscan Pasta

12 ounces uncooked pasta of your choice
Tuscan Tomato Sauce (recipe follows)
⅓ cup grated Parmesan cheese, or to taste

Cook pasta according to package directions until al dente; drain. Serve sauce over pasta. Serve with cheese. *Makes 6 servings*

Tuscan Tomato Sauce

2 tablespoons olive oil
½ cup chopped onion
2 cloves garlic, minced
8 plum tomatoes, coarsely chopped
1 can (8 ounces) tomato sauce
1 teaspoon *each* chopped fresh basil, oregano and rosemary
½ teaspoon salt
½ teaspoon black pepper

1. Heat oil in medium nonstick saucepan over medium heat. Add onion; cook and stir about 4 minutes or until tender. Add garlic; cook 1 minute more.

2. Stir in tomatoes, tomato sauce, fresh herbs, salt and pepper; bring to a boil. Reduce heat; simmer, uncovered, about 6 minutes or until desired consistency is reached, stirring occasionally. *Makes 3 cups*

Olive Lover's Pasta

Asparagus-Parmesan Risotto

5½ cups chicken broth or stock
⅛ teaspoon salt
4 tablespoons unsalted butter, divided
⅓ cup finely chopped onion
2 cups uncooked arborio rice
⅔ cup dry white wine
2½ cups fresh asparagus pieces (about 1 inch long)
⅔ cup frozen peas
1 cup grated Parmesan cheese

1. Bring broth and salt to a boil in medium saucepan over medium-high heat; reduce heat to low and simmer.

2. Meanwhile, melt 3 tablespoons butter in large saucepan over medium heat. Add onion; cook and stir 2 to 3 minutes or until tender. Stir in rice; cook, stirring frequently, 2 minutes or until most of rice grains are opaque. Add wine; cook, stirring occasionally, until most of wine evaporates.

3. Add 1½ cups broth; cook and stir 6 to 7 minutes or until most of liquid has been absorbed. (Mixture should simmer, but not boil.) Add 2 cups broth and asparagus; cook and stir 6 to 7 minutes until most of liquid has been absorbed. Add remaining 2 cups broth and peas; cook and stir 5 to 6 minutes or until most of liquid has been absorbed and rice mixture is creamy.

4. Remove from heat; stir in remaining 1 tablespoon butter and cheese until melted.

Makes 4 to 5 servings

Asparagus-Spinach Risotto: Substitute 1 cup fresh baby spinach or chopped large spinach leaves for the peas. Add the spinach at the end of step 3; cover and let stand 1 minute or until spinach is wilted. Proceed with step 4.

Asparagus-Chicken Risotto: Add 2 cups chopped or shredded cooked chicken to risotto with peas in step 3. Proceed as directed.

Tip: Broth can be added in smaller increments of ½ to ¾ cups, if desired. Just be sure to stir the rice mixture constantly for a creamy texture.

Rigatoni with Sausage & Beans

    1 pound sweet Italian sausage links, cut in ½-inch pieces
    1 jar (26 ounces) RAGÚ® Chunky Gardenstyle Pasta Sauce
    1 can (19 ounces) cannellini or white kidney beans, rinsed and drained
  ⅛ to ¼ teaspoon dried rosemary leaves, crushed (optional)
    1 box (16 ounces) rigatoni or ziti pasta, cooked and drained

1. In 12-inch skillet, brown sausage over medium-high heat; drain. Stir in Ragú Pasta Sauce, beans and rosemary.

2. Bring to a boil over high heat. Reduce heat to low and simmer uncovered, stirring occasionally, 10 minutes or until sausage is done. Serve over hot pasta.   *Makes 4 servings*

Prep Time: 5 minutes • Cook Time: 20 minutes

Quick Pasta Puttanesca

    1 package (16 ounces) uncooked spaghetti or linguine
    3 tablespoons plus 1 teaspoon olive oil, divided
  ¼ to 1 teaspoon red pepper flakes*
    2 cans (6 ounces each) chunk light tuna packed in water, drained
    1 tablespoon dried minced onion
    1 teaspoon minced garlic
    1 can (28 ounces) diced tomatoes, undrained
    1 can (8 ounces) tomato sauce
  24 pitted kalamata or ripe olives
    2 tablespoons capers, drained

For a mildly spicy dish, use ¼ teaspoon red pepper flakes. For a very spicy dish, use 1 teaspoon red pepper flakes.

1. Cook spaghetti according to package directions; drain. Return spaghetti to pan; add 1 teaspoon oil and toss to coat.

2. Meanwhile, heat remaining 3 tablespoons oil in large skillet over medium-high heat. Add red pepper flakes; cook and stir 1 to 2 minutes or until sizzling. Add tuna; cook and stir 2 to 3 minutes. Add onion and garlic; cook and stir 1 minute. Add tomatoes with juice, tomato sauce, olives and capers. Cook over medium-high heat, stirring frequently, until sauce is heated through.

3. Add sauce to pasta; mix well.   *Makes 6 to 8 servings*

Rigatoni with Sausage & Beans

Seafood Marinara with Linguine

1 pound dry linguine
2 tablespoons olive or vegetable oil, divided
1 cup chopped onion
3 large cloves garlic, minced
1 can (14½ ounces) CONTADINA® Recipe Ready Diced Tomatoes, undrained
1 can (14½ ounces) chicken broth
1 can (12 ounces) CONTADINA Tomato Paste
½ cup dry red wine or water
1 tablespoon chopped fresh basil *or* 2 teaspoons dried basil leaves, crushed
2 teaspoons chopped fresh oregano *or* ½ teaspoon dried oregano leaves, crushed
1 teaspoon salt
8 ounces fresh or frozen medium shrimp, peeled, deveined
8 ounces fresh or frozen bay scallops

1. Cook pasta according to package directions; drain and keep warm.

2. Meanwhile, heat 1 tablespoon oil in large skillet. Add onion and garlic; sauté for 2 minutes.

3. Add undrained tomatoes, broth, tomato paste, wine, basil, oregano and salt. Bring to a boil. Reduce heat to low; simmer, uncovered, for 10 minutes.

4. Heat remaining oil in small skillet. Add shrimp and scallops; sauté for 3 to 4 minutes or until shrimp turn pink.

5. Add to sauce; simmer for 2 to 3 minutes or until heated through. Serve over pasta.

Makes 6 servings

Prep Time: 12 minutes • Cook Time: 20 minutes

Seafood Marinara with Linguine

Gemelli & Roasted Summer Vegetables

2 large bell peppers (1 red and 1 yellow)
12 stalks asparagus
2 slices red onion
3 tablespoons plus 1 teaspoon olive oil, divided
6 ounces (2¼ cups) uncooked gemelli or rotini pasta
2 tablespoons pine nuts
1 clove garlic
1 cup loosely packed fresh basil leaves
¼ cup grated Parmesan cheese
¼ teaspoon salt
¼ teaspoon black pepper
1 cup grape or cherry tomatoes

1. Prepare grill for direct cooking. Cut bell peppers in half; remove and discard seeds. Place asparagus and onion on large plate; coat with 1 teaspoon olive oil.

2. Grill bell peppers, skin side down, on covered grill over medium heat 10 to 12 minutes or until skins are blackened. Place peppers in paper or plastic bag; let stand 15 minutes. Remove and discard blackened skins. Cut peppers into chunks.

3. Cook pasta according to package directions; drain and return to pan. Meanwhile, grill asparagus and onion on covered grill over medium heat 8 to 10 minutes or until tender, turning once. Cut asparagus into 2-inch pieces; cut onion into small pieces. Add bell peppers, asparagus and onion to pasta.

4. Place pine nuts and garlic in food processor. Process until coarsely chopped. Add basil; process until mixture is finely chopped. While processor is running, add remaining 3 tablespoons olive oil until mixture is blended. Stir in cheese, salt and pepper. Add basil mixture and tomatoes to pasta; toss until pasta is coated. Serve immediately.   *Makes 4 servings*

Spinach Lasagna

 5 uncooked lasagna noodles
   Nonstick cooking spray
 2 cups sliced fresh mushrooms
 1 cup chopped onion
 1 cup chopped green bell pepper
 2 cloves garlic, minced
 1 can (14½ ounces) diced tomatoes, drained
 1 can (8 ounces) tomato sauce, divided
 1 teaspoon chopped fresh basil *or* ¼ teaspoon dried basil
 1 teaspoon chopped fresh oregano *or* ¼ teaspoon dried oregano
 ⅛ teaspoon ground red pepper
1½ cups reduced-fat ricotta cheese
 ¼ cup grated Romano or Parmesan cheese
 2 egg whites
 3 tablespoons fine dry bread crumbs
 ½ (10-ounce) package frozen chopped spinach, thawed and well drained*
 ¾ cup (3 ounces) shredded part-skim mozzarella cheese
 ¼ cup chopped fresh parsley

Reserve remaining half package for another use, if desired.

1. Prepare noodles according to package directions; drain. Rinse under cold water; drain.

2. Coat large skillet with cooking spray. Add mushrooms, onion, bell pepper and garlic; cook and stir over medium heat until vegetables are tender. Stir in diced tomatoes, tomato sauce, basil, oregano and red pepper. Bring to a boil over medium-high heat. Reduce heat to medium-low. Simmer, uncovered, 10 minutes, stirring occasionally.

3. Preheat oven to 350°F. Combine ricotta cheese, Romano cheese, egg whites and bread crumbs in medium bowl. Stir spinach into ricotta mixture. Cut noodles in half crosswise. To prevent sticking, spread 2 tablespoons tomato sauce in bottom of ungreased 8-inch square baking dish. Layer 4 noodles over sauce, overlapping slightly. Top with half of cheese mixture. Layer 4 more noodles over top, slightly overlapping noodles. Top with half of tomato mixture. Repeat layers, ending with tomato sauce mixture.

4. Cover and bake 45 minutes or until hot and bubbly. Sprinkle with mozzarella cheese. Bake, uncovered, 2 to 3 minutes more or until cheese melts. Sprinkle with parsley. Let stand 10 minutes before serving.   *Makes 4 servings*

Turkey Tetrazzini with Roasted Red Peppers

6 ounces uncooked egg noodles
3 tablespoons butter
¼ cup all-purpose flour
1 can (14½ ounces) chicken broth
1 cup whipping cream
2 tablespoons dry sherry
2 cans (6 ounces each) sliced mushrooms, drained
1 jar (7½ ounces) roasted red peppers, drained and cut into ½-inch strips
2 cups chopped cooked turkey
1 teaspoon Italian seasoning
½ cup grated Parmesan cheese

1. Cook noodles according to package directions. Drain well; return noodles to pan.

2. Meanwhile, melt butter in medium saucepan over medium heat. Add flour; whisk until smooth. Add broth; bring to a boil over high heat, whisking constantly. Remove from heat. Gradually add whipping cream and sherry; stir until well blended.

3. Add mushrooms and peppers to noodles; toss well. Add half of broth mixture to noodle mixture; stir. Combine remaining broth mixture, turkey and Italian seasoning in large bowl.

4. Spoon noodle mixture into serving dish. Make a well in center of noodles; spoon turkey mixture into well. Sprinkle with cheese.

Makes 6 servings

Prep and Cook Time: 20 minutes

Turkey Tetrazzini with Roasted Red Peppers

Classic Stuffed Shells

1 jar (26 ounces) RAGÚ® Old World Style® Pasta Sauce, divided
2 pounds ricotta cheese
2 cups shredded mozzarella cheese (about 8 ounces)
¼ cup grated Parmesan cheese
3 eggs
1 tablespoon finely chopped fresh parsley
⅛ teaspoon ground black pepper
1 box (12 ounces) jumbo shells pasta, cooked and drained

Preheat oven to 350°F. In 13×9-inch baking pan, evenly spread 1 cup Ragú Old World Style Pasta Sauce; set aside.

In large bowl, combine cheeses, eggs, parsley and black pepper. Fill shells with cheese mixture, then arrange in baking pan. Evenly top with remaining sauce. Bake 45 minutes or until sauce is bubbling. *Makes 8 servings*

Tip: For a change of shape, substitute cooked and drained cannelloni or manicotti tubes for the jumbo shells. Use a teaspoon or pastry bag to fill the tubes from end to end, being careful not to overfill them.

Pasta & Potatoes with Pesto

3 medium unpeeled red potatoes, cut into chunks
8 ounces uncooked linguine
¾ cup frozen peas
1 package (about 7 ounces) prepared pesto sauce
¼ cup plus 2 tablespoons grated Parmesan cheese, divided
¼ teaspoon salt
¼ teaspoon black pepper

1. Place potatoes in medium saucepan; cover with water. Bring to a boil over high heat; reduce heat. Cook, uncovered, 10 minutes or until potatoes are tender; drain.

2. Meanwhile, cook linguine according to package directions, adding peas during last 3 minutes of cooking; drain. Return pasta mixture to pan; add potatoes, pesto sauce, ¼ cup cheese, salt and pepper, tossing until blended.

3. Serve immediately with remaining 2 tablespoons cheese. *Makes 6 servings*

Crazy Veal Bolognese Lasagna

1½ pounds ground veal
1 tablespoon olive oil
½ cup diced carrot (¼-inch dice)
½ cup diced onion (¼-inch dice)
1 cup dry red wine
1 jar (26 ounces) marinara or tomato-basil pasta sauce
1¾ cups veal stock *or* 1 can (13¾ to 14½ ounces) chicken broth
1 tablespoon finely chopped fresh parsley
1 teaspoon dried thyme leaves, crushed
1 package (20 ounces) refrigerated fresh cheese ravioli
1 container (16 ounces) refrigerated Alfredo sauce
1 cup shredded mozzarella cheese
½ cup grated Parmesan cheese
1 tablespoon finely chopped fresh parsley

1. Heat oven to 425°F. Brown ground veal in Dutch oven over medium heat 8 minutes or until veal is not pink, breaking up into small crumbles. Drain and remove veal from Dutch oven.

2. Heat oil in same Dutch oven over medium heat until hot. Add carrot and onion; cook and stir 3 to 4 minutes or until softened. Add wine; increase heat to medium-high. Cook 3 minutes or until wine is slightly reduced. Add ground veal, marinara sauce, stock, 1 tablespoon parsley and thyme; mix well. Bring to a boil. Reduce heat to maintain a gentle boil; cook 10 to 20 minutes or until mixture is reduced to 6 cups. Remove from heat.

3. Add ravioli to Dutch oven; toss to coat. Spray 13×9×2-inch baking dish or pan with nonstick cooking spray. Transfer ravioli mixture to baking dish. Spread Alfredo sauce evenly on top. Sprinkle with mozzarella and Parmesan cheeses and 1 tablespoon parsley. Cover dish and bake in 425°F oven for 20 minutes. Uncover dish; continue baking 10 minutes or until bubbly. Let stand 15 minutes before serving. *Makes 8 servings.*

Tip: If using stock, use full strength veal stock, not veal glace.

Prep and Cook Time: 1½ hours

Favorite recipe from *National Cattlemen's Beef Association on behalf of The Beef Checkoff*

Tuscan Baked Rigatoni

1 pound Italian sausage, casings removed
1 pound rigatoni pasta, cooked, drained and kept warm
2 cups (8 ounces) shredded fontina cheese
2 tablespoons olive oil
2 fennel bulbs, thinly sliced
4 cloves garlic, minced
1 can (28 ounces) crushed tomatoes
1 cup whipping cream
1 teaspoon salt
1 teaspoon black pepper
8 cups coarsely chopped fresh spinach
1 can (15 ounces) cannellini beans, rinsed and drained
2 tablespoons pine nuts
½ cup grated Parmesan cheese

1. Preheat oven to 350°F. Spray 4-quart casserole with nonstick cooking spray; set aside. Crumble sausage into large skillet over medium-high heat. Brown sausage, stirring to break up meat; drain. Transfer sausage to large bowl. Add pasta and fontina cheese; mix well.

2. Heat oil in same skillet; add fennel and garlic. Cook and stir over medium heat 3 minutes or until fennel is tender. Add tomatoes, cream, salt and pepper; cook and stir until slightly thickened. Stir in spinach, beans and pine nuts; cook until heated through.

3. Pour tomato sauce mixture over pasta and sausage; toss to coat. Transfer to prepared casserole; sprinkle evenly with Parmesan cheese. Bake 30 minutes or until hot and bubbly.

Makes 6 to 8 servings

Tuscan Baked Rigatoni

Spinach Parmesan Risotto

$3\frac{2}{3}$ cups reduced-sodium chicken broth
$\frac{1}{2}$ teaspoon white pepper
   Nonstick cooking spray
1 cup uncooked arborio rice
$1\frac{1}{2}$ cups chopped fresh spinach
$\frac{1}{2}$ cup fresh or frozen green peas
1 tablespoon minced fresh dill *or* 1 teaspoon dried dill weed
$\frac{1}{2}$ cup grated Parmesan cheese
1 teaspoon grated lemon peel

1. Combine chicken broth and pepper in medium saucepan; bring to a boil over medium-high heat. Reduce heat and continue simmering.

2. Spray large saucepan with cooking spray; heat over medium-low heat until hot. Add rice; cook and stir 1 minute. Stir $\frac{2}{3}$ cup broth into saucepan; cook, stirring constantly, until broth is absorbed.

3. Stir remaining broth into rice mixture, $\frac{1}{2}$ cup at a time, stirring constantly until all broth is absorbed before adding next $\frac{1}{2}$ cup. When last $\frac{1}{2}$ cup broth is added, stir in spinach, peas and dill. Cook, stirring gently until all broth is absorbed and rice is tender but firm. (Total cooking time is about 20 minutes.)

4. Remove saucepan from heat; stir in cheese and lemon peel.   *Makes 6 servings*

Creamy Pancetta Rice

$\frac{1}{2}$ pound trimmed pancetta, diced
1 large red onion, chopped
$1\frac{3}{4}$ cups half-and-half
3 cups cooked rice
$1\frac{1}{2}$ cups sweetened, dried cranberries
1 cup chopped pistachio nuts
$\frac{1}{2}$ teaspoon salt
$\frac{1}{4}$ teaspoon ground black pepper

Brown pancetta and onion in large skillet over medium heat; cook until onion begins to brown, about 8 minutes. Add half-and-half; bring to a boil. Remove from heat. Add rice, cranberries, pistachios, salt and pepper. Stir until well blended.   *Makes 8 servings*

Favorite recipe from **USA Rice**

Spinach Parmesan Risotto

Beef, Pork and Veal

page 98

page 90

page 94

Italy is famous for its veal and pork dishes–veal scallopine, veal parmigiana, pork piccata and an astonishing array of sausages. Beef is less common but it is enjoyed in meatballs, Bolognese sauce and braciola. Serve a traditional Italian meat specialty, or try something new, such as Tuscan Steak or Pork Chops with Balsamic Vinegar, and you'll get plenty of raves.

Tuscan Beef

pictured on page 85

>   1 tablespoon olive oil
>   2 cloves garlic, minced
> 1½ teaspoons dried rosemary, divided
>   1 teaspoon salt
>   ½ teaspoon black pepper
>   4 boneless beef rib eye or strip steaks (8 to 10 ounces each, ¾- to 1-inch thick)
>   ¾ cup prepared marinara or tomato-basil pasta sauce
>   ½ cup sliced pimiento-stuffed olives
>   1 tablespoon drained capers

1. Prepare grill for direct cooking or preheat broiler. Combine oil, garlic, 1 teaspoon rosemary, salt and pepper in small bowl; mix well. Spread mixture evenly over both sides of steaks.

2. Grill steaks, covered, over medium-hot coals or broil 4 inches from heat source 4 to 5 minutes per side for medium-rare (150°F internal temperature) or to desired doneness.

3. Meanwhile, combine pasta sauce, olives, capers and remaining ½ teaspoon rosemary in small saucepan; mix well. Heat until hot but not boiling. Transfer steaks to serving plates; top with sauce.

Makes 4 servings

Ragú® Steak Pizzaiola

>   4 rib-eye round steaks (1½ pounds)
>   2 teaspoons finely chopped garlic
>   4 tablespoons grated Parmesan cheese
>   ½ teaspoon salt
>   ½ teaspoon ground black pepper
>   2 cups frozen French-cut green beans, thawed
>   1 jar (26 ounces) RAGÚ® Robusto!® Pasta Sauce

Preheat oven to 400°F. In bottom of 13×9-inch baking pan, arrange steaks; sprinkle with garlic, 2 tablespoons of the Parmesan cheese, salt and pepper. Add green beans and Ragú Robusto! Pasta Sauce. Bake 20 minutes or until desired doneness. Sprinkle with remaining cheese. Serve, if desired, over hot cooked noodles.

Makes 4 servings

Grilled Veal Chops with Sage Jus and Gorgonzola Polenta

4 veal loin or rib chops, cut 1 inch thick
¼ cup olive oil
¼ cup whole fresh sage leaves
4 cloves garlic, smashed
1 cup veal stock or beef broth
  Salt and pepper
  Chopped fresh sage (optional)

Gorgonzola Polenta:
1½ cups milk
½ cup water
⅔ cup coarse grind yellow cornmeal
3 tablespoons mascarpone
1 tablespoon crumbled Gorgonzola
1 tablespoon butter
½ teaspoon salt
⅛ teaspoon black pepper

1. Combine ¼ cup oil, whole sage and garlic in heavy small saucepan. Bring to a simmer over low heat; simmer 30 minutes. Strain out solids. Set aside. Clean out saucepan.

2. Bring stock to a boil in same saucepan over high heat. Reduce heat to medium; simmer 22 to 24 minutes or until reduced by half. Add sage oil; simmer 1 minute. Season sage jus with salt and pepper, as desired. Set aside; keep warm.

3. Season each veal chop with salt and pepper as desired. Place chops on grid over medium, ash-covered coals. Grill, uncovered, 12 to 14 minutes for medium doneness, turning once.

4. Meanwhile prepare Gorgonzola polenta. Combine milk and water in large saucepan. Bring to a boil; reduce heat to a simmer. Pour cornmeal very slowly in thin stream into milk mixture, whisking constantly to prevent clumps. Cook and stir over low heat 10 minutes or until polenta thickens and pulls away from side of pan. Remove from heat; stir in mascarpone, Gorgonzola, butter, salt and pepper.

5. Serve each chop with 2 tablespoons sage jus and ½ cup polenta. Garnish with chopped sage, if desired. *Makes 4 servings.*

Prep and Cook Time: 30 minutes

Favorite recipe from **National Cattlemen's Beef Association on behalf of The Beef Checkoff**

Braciola

1 can (28 ounces) tomato sauce
2½ teaspoons dried oregano, divided
1¼ teaspoons dried basil, divided
1 teaspoon salt
½ pound bulk hot Italian sausage or hot Italian sausages, casings removed
½ cup chopped onion
¼ cup grated Parmesan cheese
2 cloves garlic, minced
1 tablespoon dried parsley flakes
1 to 2 beef flank steaks (about 2½ pounds)

Slow Cooker Directions

1. Combine tomato sauce, 2 teaspoons oregano, 1 teaspoon basil and salt in medium bowl; set aside.

2. Brown sausage in large nonstick skillet over medium-high heat, stirring to break up meat. Drain fat. Combine sausage, onion, cheese, garlic, parsley, remaining ½ teaspoon oregano and remaining ¼ teaspoon basil in medium bowl; set aside.

3. Place steak between 2 pieces waxed paper. Pound with meat mallet until steak is ⅛ to ¼ inch thick. Cut steak into 3-inch-wide strips.

4. Spoon sausage mixture evenly onto each steak strip. Roll up, jelly-roll-style, securing meat with toothpicks. Place each roll in slow cooker. Pour reserved tomato sauce mixture over rolls. Cover; cook on LOW 6 to 8 hours or until meat is tender.

5. Cut each roll into slices. Top with hot tomato sauce.

Makes 8 servings

Prep Time: 35 minutes • Cook Time: 6 to 8 hours

Braciola can also be made with boneless top round steak (about 2 ½ pounds). Purchase a steak about ½ inch thick and pound it until it is about ¼ inch thick. Cut the steak into 8 strips. Proceed as directed in step 4.

Baked Italian Meatballs

   1 pound ground beef (90% to 95% lean)
   ¼ cup seasoned dry bread crumbs
   1 egg
   2 tablespoons water
   1 teaspoon minced garlic
   ½ teaspoon salt
   ⅛ teaspoon pepper
   1 jar (14½ ounces) pasta sauce, heated
      Hot cooked pasta or crusty Italian rolls (optional)

1. Heat oven to 400°F. Combine ground beef, bread crumbs, egg, water, garlic, salt and pepper in large bowl, mixing lightly but thoroughly. Shape into 12 two-inch meatballs. Place on rack in broiler pan. Bake in 400°F oven 17 to 19 minutes to medium (160°F) doneness, until not pink in center and juices show no pink color.

2. Serve with pasta sauce over hot cooked pasta or as sandwiches in crusty Italian rolls, if desired.

Makes 4 servings.

Prep and Cook Time: 30 to 35 minutes

Favorite recipe from ***National Cattlemen's Beef Association on behalf of The Beef Checkoff***

Grilled Italian Steak

   1 cup WISH-BONE® Italian Dressing*
   3 tablespoons grated Parmesan cheese
   3 teaspoons dried basil leaves, crushed
   ¼ teaspoon cracked black pepper
   2 to 3-pound boneless sirloin or top round steak

*Also terrific with WISH-BONE® Robusto Italian Dressing.

In small bowl, combine all ingredients except steak.

In nonaluminum baking dish or plastic bag, pour ¾ cup marinade over steak. Cover or close bag and marinate in refrigerator, turning occasionally, 3 to 24 hours. Refrigerate remaining marinade.

Remove steak from marinade, discarding marinade. Grill or broil steak, turning once, and brushing frequently with reserved marinade, until steak is desired doneness.   *Makes 8 servings*

Prep Time: 5 minutes • **Marinate Time:** 3 hours • **Cook Time:** 15 minutes

Classic Veal Florentine

6 ounces fresh spinach, chopped
6 tablespoons butter, divided
2 cloves garlic, minced
1 can (14½ ounces) whole peeled tomatoes, undrained
¼ cup dry white wine
¼ cup water
1 tablespoon tomato paste
¾ teaspoon salt, divided
½ teaspoon sugar
¼ teaspoon black pepper, divided
¼ cup all-purpose flour
4 veal cutlets (⅜ inch thick, about 4 ounces each)
1 tablespoon olive oil
1 cup (4 ounces) shredded mozzarella cheese
   Hot cooked pasta (optional)

1. Place spinach in large saucepan over medium heat. Cover and steam 4 minutes or until tender, stirring occasionally. Add 2 tablespoons butter; cook and stir until butter is absorbed. Remove from saucepan; set aside.

2. To make tomato sauce, heat 2 tablespoons butter in medium saucepan over medium heat until melted and bubbly. Add garlic; cook and stir 30 seconds. Press tomatoes with juice through sieve into garlic mixture; discard seeds. Add wine, water, tomato paste, ½ teaspoon salt, sugar and ⅛ teaspoon pepper to tomato mixture. Bring to a boil; reduce heat to low. Simmer, uncovered, 10 minutes, stirring occasionally. Remove from heat; set aside.

3. Mix flour, remaining ¼ teaspoon salt and ⅛ teaspoon pepper in small resealable food storage bag. Pound veal with meat mallet to ¼-inch thickness. Pat dry with paper towels. Shake veal, one cutlet at a time, in seasoned flour to coat evenly.

4. Heat oil and remaining 2 tablespoons butter in large skillet over medium heat until bubbly. Add veal to skillet; cook 2 to 3 minutes per side until light brown. Remove from heat. Spoon off excess fat. Top veal with reserved spinach and cheese.

5. Pour tomato mixture into skillet, lifting edges of veal to let sauce flow underneath. Cook over low heat until bubbly. Cover and simmer 8 minutes or until heated through. Serve with pasta.

Makes 4 servings

Steak with Arugula & Gorgonzola Salad

    4 beef top loin steaks (¾ inch thick)
    1 cup balsamic or red wine salad dressing, divided
   16 large arugula leaves *or* 1½ cups baby arugula leaves
  1½ cups mixed salad greens
   ⅓ cup crumbled Gorgonzola cheese

1. Place steaks in resealable food storage bag; pour ½ cup salad dressing into bag. Seal bag; turn to coat. Marinate 20 minutes. Meanwhile, prepare grill for direct cooking.

2. Remove steaks from marinade; discard marinade. Grill steaks over medium-high heat 3 to 4 minutes on each side for medium-rare or until desired doneness.

3. Meanwhile, combine arugula and salad greens. Pour remaining ½ cup dressing over greens; toss until greens are well coated. Serve steaks with salad. Sprinkle cheese over salad and steaks.

Makes 4 servings

Pork Piccata

    1 pork tenderloin, about 1 pound
    3 tablespoons all-purpose flour
    2 teaspoons lemon pepper
    2 teaspoons butter
   ¼ cup dry sherry or white wine
   ¼ cup lemon juice
    4 to 6 thick lemon slices
    4 tablespoons capers

Slice tenderloin into 8 equal pieces; flatten each piece gently to a scallop with thickness of ⅛ inch. Dredge scallops lightly with flour; sprinkle with lemon pepper. Melt butter in nonstick skillet over medium-high heat. Quickly sauté scallops, turning once, until golden brown, about 4 to 5 minutes. Add sherry and lemon juice to skillet; shake skillet gently and cook 2 minutes, until sauce is slightly thickened. Serve garnished with lemon slices and capers.

Makes 4 servings

Prep Time: 15 minutes

Favorite recipe from **National Pork Board**

Steak with Arugula & Gorgonzola Salad

Italian Sausage and Peppers

3 cups bell pepper chunks, preferably a mix of red, yellow and green*
1 small onion, cut into thin wedges
3 cloves garlic, minced
4 links hot or mild Italian sausage (about 1 pound)
1 cup marinara sauce or pasta sauce
¼ cup red wine or port
1 tablespoon cornstarch
1 tablespoon water
Hot cooked spaghetti
¼ cup grated Parmesan or Romano cheese

*Look for mixed bell pepper chunks at your supermarket salad bar.

Slow Cooker Directions

1. Coat slow cooker with cooking spray. Place bell peppers, onion and garlic in slow cooker. Arrange sausage over vegetables. Combine marinara sauce and wine; pour over sausage. Cover; cook on LOW 8 to 9 hours or on HIGH 4 to 5 hours.

2. Transfer sausage to serving platter; cover with foil to keep warm. Skim off and discard fat from juices in slow cooker.

3. Turn heat to HIGH. Mix cornstarch with water until smooth; add to slow cooker. Cook 15 minutes or until sauce is thickened, stirring once. Serve sauce over spaghetti and sausage; top with cheese.   *Makes 4 servings*

Cook Time: 8¼ to 9¼ hours

Stuffed Pork Loin Genoa Style

    1 (4- to 5-pound) boneless pork loin roast
 1¼ cups fresh parsley sprigs, chopped and divided
  ½ cup fresh basil leaves, chopped
  ½ cup pine nuts
  ½ cup grated Parmesan cheese
   6 cloves garlic, peeled and chopped
  ½ pound ground pork
  ½ pound Italian sausage
   1 cup dry bread crumbs
  ¼ cup milk
   1 egg
   1 teaspoon ground black pepper

In food processor or blender, process 1 cup parsley, basil, pine nuts, Parmesan cheese and garlic. Set aside.

Mix together ground pork, Italian sausage, bread crumbs, milk, egg, remaining ¼ cup parsley and pepper.

Place roast fat-side down on cutting board. Spread with the herb-cheese mixture; place ground pork mixture along center of loin. Fold in half; tie with kitchen string. Roast on rack in shallow baking pan at 350°F for 1½ hours or until internal temperature reaches 155°F. Slice to serve.

Makes 10 servings

Prep Time: 15 minutes • Cook Time: 90 minutes

Favorite recipe from **National Pork Board**

Osso Buco

   3 pounds veal shanks (about 4 shanks)
   ¾ teaspoon salt, divided
   ½ teaspoon black pepper
   ½ cup all-purpose flour
   2 tablespoons olive oil
   1 cup finely chopped carrot
   1 cup chopped onion
   1 cup finely chopped celery
   2 cloves garlic, minced
   ½ cup dry white wine
   1 can (14½ ounces) diced tomatoes, undrained
   1 cup beef broth
   1 tablespoon chopped fresh basil or rosemary
   1 bay leaf
     Parmesan Gremolata (recipe follows)
   1 package (about 5½ ounces) risotto (optional)

1. Season veal shanks with ½ teaspoon salt and pepper. Place flour in shallow bowl; dredge veal shanks, one at a time, shaking off excess.

2. Heat oil in large ovenproof Dutch oven over medium-high heat. Brown veal shanks 20 minutes, turning one-quarter turn every 5 minutes. Remove to plate.

3. Preheat oven to 350°F. Add carrot, onion, celery and garlic to Dutch oven; cook and stir 5 minutes or until vegetables are soft. To deglaze Dutch oven, pour wine over carrot mixture. Cook over medium-high heat 2 to 3 minutes, stirring to scrape up any browned bits.

4. Add tomatoes with juice, broth, basil, bay leaf and remaining ¼ teaspoon salt to Dutch oven; bring to a boil. Return veal shanks to Dutch oven; cover and bake 2 hours.

5. Meanwhile, prepare Parmesan Gremolata and risotto.

6. Remove bay leaf; discard. Remove veal shanks to individual serving bowls; spoon vegetable mixture over each serving. Sprinkle with Parmesan Gremolata. Serve with risotto.   *Makes 4 to 6 servings*

Parmesan Gremolata

     Grated peel of 1 lemon
   ⅓ cup grated Parmesan cheese
   ¼ cup chopped fresh parsley
   1 clove garlic, minced

Combine lemon peel, cheese, parsley and garlic in small bowl. Cover and refrigerate until ready to use.   *Makes about ⅓ cup*

Italian Cheese Steaks

　　4 boneless sirloin steaks (6 to 8 ounces each)
　　1 tablespoon olive oil
　　1 jar (26 ounces) RAGÚ® ROBUSTO!® Pasta Sauce
　　⅛ to ¼ teaspoon crushed red pepper flakes (optional)
　　1 cup shredded mozzarella cheese (about 4 ounces)

1. Season steaks, if desired, with salt and ground black pepper.

2. In 12-inch skillet, heat olive oil over medium-high heat and brown steaks, turning occasionally, 4 minutes or until steaks are almost done. Remove steaks and set aside.

3. In same skillet, stir in Pasta Sauce and red pepper flakes. Cook, stirring frequently, 2 minutes. Return steaks to skillet; top steaks with cheese. Cook, covered, over medium heat 2 minutes or until cheese is melted. To serve, arrange steaks on platter. Pour Sauce around steaks and garnish, if desired, with chopped fresh parsley.　　　　　　　　　　　　　　　*Makes 4 servings*

Prep Time: 5 minutes • **Cook Time:** 10 minutes

Beef Sirloin in Rich Italian Sauce

　　2 tablespoons olive or vegetable oil
　　1 pound top sirloin, cut into thin strips
　　2 cloves garlic, cut in half
　　1 can (14½ ounces) CONTADINA® Recipe Ready Diced Tomatoes, undrained
　　2 tablespoons chopped fresh parsley *or* 2 teaspoons dried parsley flakes
　　2 tablespoons dry red wine or beef broth
　　½ teaspoon dried thyme leaves, crushed
　　¼ teaspoon dried rosemary leaves, crushed
　　¼ teaspoon salt
　　¼ teaspoon ground black pepper
　　　　Additional chopped fresh parsley (optional)

1. Heat oil over high heat in large skillet. Add meat and garlic; cook for 1 to 2 minutes or until meat is browned, stirring occasionally. Remove meat from skillet; discard garlic.

2. Add undrained tomatoes, parsley, wine, thyme, rosemary, salt and pepper to skillet; stir. Bring to a boil. Reduce heat to low.

3. Return meat to skillet; cover. Simmer for 5 minutes. Sprinkle with additional fresh parsley, if desired.　　　　　　　　　　　　　　　*Makes 4 servings*

Prep Time: 8 minutes • **Cook Time:** 9 minutes

Italian Cheese Steak

Pork Chops with Balsamic Vinegar

   2 boneless center pork loin chops, 1½ inches thick
1½ teaspoons lemon pepper
   1 teaspoon vegetable oil
   3 tablespoons balsamic vinegar
   2 tablespoons chicken broth
   2 teaspoons butter

Pat chops dry. Coat with lemon pepper. Heat oil in heavy skillet over medium-high heat. Add chops. Brown on first side 8 minutes; turn and cook 7 minutes more or until done. Remove from pan and keep warm. Add vinegar and broth to skillet; cook, stirring, until syrupy (about 1 to 2 minutes). Stir in butter until blended. Spoon sauce over chops.   *Makes 2 servings*

Prep Time: 20 minutes

Favorite recipe from **National Pork Board**

Mushroom and Sausage Ragu on Soft Polenta

   ½ **pound (8 ounces) Italian sausage links**
    2 **tablespoons olive oil**
1½ **pounds mushrooms, sliced (about 5 cups)**
1½ **cups tomato-based pasta sauce**
    1 **teaspoon red wine vinegar**
   ½ **cup instant polenta**
   ½ **teaspoon salt**
   ¼ **teaspoon pepper**

In a large (12-inch) skillet, over medium-high heat, combine sausages and 2 tablespoons water. Cook and stir until browned on all sides, about 12 minutes; remove sausages and drain on paper towels. Drain grease. Add olive oil to pan; cook mushrooms until lightly browned and liquid has evaporated, about 12 minutes. Cut sausage into ¼-inch slices; add to skillet with pasta sauce, vinegar and water as needed to thin sauce. Reduce heat to low. Simmer until hot, about 5 minutes. Meanwhile, in a large microwavable bowl, combine polenta and 1 cup water; whisk until smooth. Gradually whisk in 1½ cups water, salt and pepper until smooth.* Microwave on HIGH 4 minutes. Whisk until mixture is well blended; microwave until smooth, about 4 minutes longer. Serve mushroom and sausage ragu over polenta. Garnish with thinly sliced fresh basil leaves if desired.

For polenta with a creamy texture, substitute 1½ cups chicken broth and 1 cup milk for the water; omit salt.

Favorite recipe from **Mushroom Council**

Pork Chop with Balsamic Vinegar

Veal Parmigiana

4 veal cutlets or veal scallopine (⅜ inch thick, about 4 ounces each)
4 tablespoons olive oil, divided
1 small red bell pepper, finely chopped
1 medium onion, finely chopped
1 stalk celery, finely chopped
1 clove garlic, minced
1 can (14½ ounces) whole tomatoes, undrained and finely chopped
1 cup chicken broth
1 tablespoon chopped fresh parsley
1 tablespoon tomato paste
1 teaspoon sugar
¾ teaspoon dried basil
½ teaspoon salt
⅛ teaspoon black pepper
1 egg
¼ cup all-purpose flour
⅔ cup fine dry bread crumbs
2 tablespoons butter
1½ cups (about 6 ounces) shredded mozzarella cheese
⅔ cup grated Parmesan cheese
Fresh basil leaves (optional)

1. Pound veal with meat mallet to ¼-inch thickness; pat dry with paper towels. Set aside.

2. To make tomato sauce, heat 1 tablespoon oil in medium saucepan over medium heat. Add bell pepper, onion, celery and garlic; cook and stir 5 minutes. Stir in tomatoes with juice, broth, parsley, tomato paste, sugar, dried basil, salt and black pepper. Cover; simmer over low heat 20 minutes. Uncover; cook over medium heat 20 minutes or until sauce thickens, stirring frequently. Set aside.

3. Beat egg in shallow bowl. Spread flour and bread crumbs on separate plates. Dip veal cutlets to coat both sides evenly, first in flour, then in egg, then in bread crumbs. Press crumb coating firmly onto veal.

4. Heat butter and 2 tablespoons oil in large skillet over medium-high heat. Add veal. Cook 3 minutes per side or until browned.

5. Preheat oven to 350°F. Remove veal with slotted spatula to ungreased 13×9-inch baking dish. Sprinkle mozzarella cheese evenly over veal. Spoon tomato sauce evenly over mozzarella cheese. Sprinkle Parmesan cheese over tomato sauce. Drizzle remaining 1 tablespoon oil over top.

6. Bake, uncovered, 25 minutes or until veal is tender and cheese is golden. Garnish with basil leaves.

Makes 4 servings

Pork Medallions with Marsala

1 pound pork tenderloin, cut into ½-inch slices
All-purpose flour
2 tablespoons olive oil
1 clove garlic, minced
½ cup sweet marsala wine
2 tablespoons chopped fresh parsley

1. Lightly dredge pork in flour. Heat oil in large skillet over medium-high heat. Add pork; cook 3 minutes per side or until browned. Remove from pan. Reduce heat to medium.

2. Add garlic to skillet; cook and stir 1 minute. Add wine and pork; cook 3 minutes or until pork is barely pink in center. Remove pork from skillet. Stir in parsley. Simmer wine mixture 2 to 3 minutes or until slightly thickened. Serve over pork.   *Makes 4 servings*

Tip: For a special touch, sprinkle with chopped red onion just before serving.

Tuscan Pork with Peppers

1 pound boneless pork chops, cut into 1-inch cubes
1 medium onion, peeled and chopped
2 cloves garlic, minced
1 teaspoon olive oil
1 (14½-ounce) can Italian-style tomatoes, undrained
½ cup dry white wine
1 sweet red bell pepper, seeded and sliced
1 green bell pepper, seeded and sliced

Sauté pork cubes, onion and garlic in olive oil in large nonstick skillet over medium-high heat until pork starts to brown, about 4 to 5 minutes. Add remaining ingredients; lower heat to a simmer. Cover and cook gently for 12 to 15 minutes. Taste for seasoning, adding salt and black pepper, if desired. Serve with hot cooked rigatoni or penne, if desired.   *Makes 4 servings*

Prep Time: 30 minutes

Favorite recipe from **National Pork Board**

Veal Scallopine

4 veal cutlets or veal scallopine (⅜ inch thick, about 4 ounces each)
¼ cup (½ stick) butter
½ pound fresh mushrooms, thinly sliced
2 tablespoons olive oil
1 small onion, finely chopped
¼ cup dry sherry
2 teaspoons all-purpose flour
½ cup beef broth
¼ teaspoon salt
⅛ teaspoon black pepper
2 tablespoons whipping cream
Hot cooked pasta

1. Pound veal with meat mallet to ¼-inch thickness; pat dry with paper towels. Set aside.

2. Heat butter in large skillet over medium-high heat until melted and bubbly. Add mushrooms; cook and stir 3 to 4 minutes or until lightly browned. Remove mushrooms with slotted spoon; set aside.

3. Add oil to butter in skillet; heat over medium heat. Add veal; cook 2 to 3 minutes per side or until light brown. Remove veal; reserve.

4. Add onion to same skillet; cook and stir 2 to 3 minutes or until soft. Stir in sherry; boil over medium-high heat 15 seconds. Stir in flour; cook and stir 30 seconds. Stir in broth; bring to a boil over medium heat, stirring constantly. Stir in mushrooms, salt and pepper. Add veal to sauce mixture; reduce heat to low. Cover; simmer 8 minutes or until veal is tender. Remove from heat.

5. Remove veal to serving plates. Stir cream into sauce mixture. Cook over low heat until heated through. Serve over pasta and veal. *Makes 4 servings*

Cooking mushrooms helps develop their flavor. This is best done over medium-high heat with constant stirring. If mushrooms are cooked at too low a temperature, they will not brown and develop their characteristic intense flavor.

Italian Porketta

   2 to 4 pounds boneless pork roast
   3 tablespoons dill seed
   1 tablespoon fennel seed
   1 teaspoon lemon pepper
   ¼ teaspoon onion powder
   ¼ teaspoon garlic powder
   ¼ teaspoon oregano

Combine seasonings together and coat roast with mixture. Roast in shallow pan at 325°F for 45 minutes to 1 hour, until meat thermometer registers 155° to 160°F. Let roast rest 5 to 10 minutes before carving.   *Makes 8 to 12 servings*

Prep Time: 5 minutes • **Cook Time:** 60 minutes

Favorite recipe from **National Pork Board**

Piedmont Pork Stew

   1 pound boneless pork loin, cut into 1-inch cubes
   1 teaspoon vegetable oil
   1 medium onion, coarsely chopped
   2 carrots, sliced
   8 ounces mushrooms, chopped
   1 can (8 ounces) tomato sauce
   1 cup dry red wine
   ½ cup raisins
   1 teaspoon dried thyme leaves
   1 teaspoon dried oregano leaves
   ¼ teaspoon ground cinnamon
   ¼ teaspoon salt
      Hot cooked rice or orzo (optional)

Brown pork in oil in large pot over medium-high heat until browned, about 3 minutes. Add remaining ingredients except rice and bring to a boil; reduce heat to a simmer, cover and cook gently 15 to 20 minutes. Serve over rice, if desired.   *Makes 6 servings*

Prep Time: 30 minutes

Favorite recipe from **National Pork Board**

Italian Porketta

Chicken and Turkey

page 126

page 136

page 142

Discover more than twenty tasty recipes in this chapter and savor the goodness of chicken and turkey paired with simple, fresh ingredients like tomatoes, Parmesan cheese, spinach, mushrooms, prosciutto, rosemary, basil, garlic, wine and pesto sauce. You'll be surprised how easy it is to create fabulous, flavorful dinners that everyone will love.

Chicken Tuscany

pictured on page 115

> 6 medium red potatoes, scrubbed and sliced ⅛ inch thick
> 12 ounces shiitake, cremini, chanterelle and/or button mushrooms, sliced
> 4 tablespoons olive oil, divided
> 4 tablespoons grated Parmesan cheese, divided
> 3 teaspoons minced garlic, divided
> 3 teaspoons minced fresh rosemary *or* 1½ teaspoons dried rosemary leaves, divided
>   Salt and ground black pepper
> 1 package (about 3 pounds) PERDUE® Fresh Pick of the Chicken

Preheat oven to 425°F. Pat potatoes dry with paper towels. Toss potatoes and mushrooms with 2½ tablespoons oil, 2 tablespoons cheese, 2 teaspoons garlic, 2 teaspoons rosemary, ½ teaspoon salt and ¼ teaspoon pepper. In 13×9-inch baking dish, arrange potatoes in one layer; top with remaining 2 tablespoons cheese. Bake 15 minutes or until potatoes are lightly browned; set aside.

Meanwhile, in large nonstick skillet over medium heat, heat remaining 1½ tablespoons oil. Add chicken pieces. Season lightly with salt and pepper; sprinkle with remaining 1 teaspoon rosemary and garlic. Cook chicken 5 to 6 minutes on each side or until browned. (Do not crowd pan; if necessary, brown chicken in two batches.)

Arrange chicken on top of potato mixture; drizzle with oil from skillet and return to oven. Bake 20 to 25 minutes longer or until chicken is no longer pink in center. Serve chicken, potatoes and mushrooms with green salad, if desired. *Makes 6 servings*

Chicken with Smoked Ham & Provolone

> 4 boneless skinless chicken breasts
>   Salt and black pepper
> ¼ teaspoon Italian seasoning
> 1 tablespoon olive oil
> 2 slices provolone cheese, cut into quarters
> 4 thin slices smoked deli ham

1. Pound chicken between two sheets of waxed paper until ½ inch thick. Season with salt, pepper and Italian seasoning.

2. Heat olive oil in large nonstick skillet over medium-high heat. Add chicken; cook 4 to 5 minutes on each side until no longer pink in center. Top each chicken breast with 2 cheese pieces and ham slice, folding ham to fit. Cover and heat 1 to 2 minutes or just until cheese melts. Garnish with fresh basil leaves. *Makes 4 servings*

Tuscan Turkey Cutlets

1 pound turkey cutlets
¾ teaspoon salt, divided
¾ teaspoon black pepper, divided
1 tablespoon olive oil, divided
2 cups coarsely chopped onions
1 cup coarsely chopped carrots
3 to 4 cloves garlic, minced
½ teaspoon dried oregano
⅓ teaspoon dried thyme
1 (10-ounce) bag fresh spinach leaves, stems removed
1 (14½-ounce) can diced tomatoes, undrained
1 (19-ounce) can cannellini beans, drained and rinsed
¼ cup grated Parmesan cheese

1. Place cutlets on cutting board and sprinkle with ¼ teaspoon salt and ¼ teaspoon pepper. Slice cutlets into ½-inch strips.

2. In 12-inch or larger nonstick skillet over medium-high heat, sauté turkey strips in ½ tablespoon oil 4 to 5 minutes or until no longer pink (165°F). Remove from skillet; set aside.

3. Add remaining ½ tablespoon oil to skillet. Sauté onions, carrots, garlic, oregano and thyme 5 minutes or until vegetables are tender. Gradually add spinach and stir an additional 2 minutes or until spinach is wilted, but not quite done. Add tomatoes and remaining ½ teaspoon salt and ½ teaspoon pepper; cook 2 minutes.

4. Stir in turkey strips and beans. Cook until heated through.

5. Serve topped with Parmesan cheese.

Makes 4 servings

Serving Suggestion: Serve over orzo, noodles or a whole grain such as quinoa.

Favorite recipe from **National Turkey Federation**

Cannellini beans are also known as white kidney beans. Great Northern beans can be substituted if cannellini beans are unavailable.

Turkey Roulade

1 pound (10 slices) uncooked, boneless turkey breast
1 container (15 ounces) ricotta cheese
1½ cups (6 ounces) shredded mozzarella cheese, divided
1 package (10 ounces) frozen chopped spinach, thawed, squeezed dry
1 teaspoon garlic salt
1 tablespoon olive or vegetable oil
1 cup chopped onion
2 cloves garlic, minced
1 can (14½ ounces) CONTADINA® Recipe Ready Diced Tomatoes, undrained
1 can (6 ounces) CONTADINA Tomato Paste
1 cup chicken broth
1 teaspoon Italian herb seasoning
1 teaspoon salt
1 teaspoon ground black pepper

1. Pound turkey slices between 2 pieces of plastic wrap to ⅛-inch thickness.

2. Combine ricotta cheese, 1 cup mozzarella cheese, spinach and garlic salt in medium bowl. Spread ⅓ cup cheese mixture onto each turkey slice; roll up. Secure with toothpick. Place rolls in 13×9-inch baking dish.

3. Heat oil in large skillet. Add onion and garlic; sauté for 2 minutes. Add undrained tomatoes, tomato paste, broth, Italian seasoning, salt and pepper. Bring to a boil.

4. Reduce heat to low; simmer for 10 minutes. Spoon sauce over rolls; cover.

5. Bake in preheated 425°F oven for 20 to 25 minutes or until turkey is no longer pink in center. Sprinkle with remaining ½ cup mozzarella cheese. Bake for additional 5 minutes or until cheese is melted. *Makes 10 servings*

Prep Time: 20 minutes • Cook Time: 43 minutes

Chicken & Mushrooms with Pasta & Roasted Garlic Sauce

- 1 teaspoon olive oil
- 4 boneless skinless chicken breasts
- 1 jar (about 28 ounces) roasted garlic pasta sauce
- 1 cup sliced mushrooms
- 8 ounces uncooked rotini or fusilli pasta, cooked and drained
  Grated Parmesan cheese (optional)

1. Heat oil in large skillet over medium heat. Lightly brown chicken. Remove from skillet; cut into thin strips. Return to skillet.

2. Stir in pasta sauce and mushrooms. Cover; simmer 10 minutes or until chicken is cooked through. Stir in pasta. Sprinkle with cheese, if desired. *Makes 4 servings*

Sicilian Skillet Chicken

- 4 boneless, skinless chicken breast halves
- 6 tablespoons grated Parmesan cheese, divided
- 3 tablespoons all-purpose flour
- 2 tablespoons olive oil
- 1 cup sliced mushrooms
- ½ medium onion, finely chopped
- ½ teaspoon dried rosemary, crushed
- 1 can (14½ ounces) DEL MONTE® Diced Tomatoes with Basil, Garlic & Oregano

1. Slightly flatten each chicken breast. Coat breasts with 4 tablespoons cheese and flour. Season with salt and pepper, if desired.

2. Heat oil in large skillet over medium-high heat. Cook chicken until no longer pink, turning once. Remove to serving dish; keep warm.

3. Cook mushrooms, onion and rosemary in same skillet over medium-high heat until tender. Add tomatoes; cook, uncovered, over medium-high heat until thickened.

4. Spoon over chicken; top with remaining 2 tablespoons cheese. Serve with pasta and garnish with chopped parsley, if desired. *Makes 4 servings*

Prep Time: 5 minutes • Cook Time: 25 minutes

Spinach, Cheese and Prosciutto-Stuffed Chicken Breasts

    4 boneless skinless chicken breasts (about 4 ounces each)
       Salt and black pepper
    4 slices (½ ounce each) prosciutto*
    4 slices (½ ounce each) smoked provolone**
    1 cup spinach leaves, chopped
    4 tablespoons all-purpose flour, divided
    1 tablespoon olive oil
    1 tablespoon butter
    1 cup chicken broth
    1 tablespoon heavy whipping cream

*Thinly sliced deli ham can be substituted for the prosciutto.

**Mozzarella cheese may be substituted for the smoked provolone.

1. Preheat oven to 350°F.

2. To form pocket, cut each chicken breast horizontally almost to opposite edge. Fold back top half of chicken breast; sprinkle chicken lightly with salt and pepper. Place 1 slice prosciutto, 1 slice provolone and ¼ cup spinach on each chicken breast. Fold top half of breasts over filling.

3. Lightly sprinkle chicken with salt and pepper. Spread 3 tablespoons flour on plate. Holding chicken breast closed, coat with flour; shake off excess.

4. Heat oil and butter in large skillet over medium heat. Place chicken in skillet; cook about 4 minutes on each side or until browned.

5. Transfer chicken to shallow baking dish. Do not wash skillet; reserve to make sauce. Bake 10 minutes or until chicken is no longer pink in center.

6. Whisk chicken broth and cream into remaining 1 tablespoon flour in small bowl. Pour chicken broth mixture into reserved skillet; heat about 3 minutes over medium heat, stirring constantly, until sauce thickens. Spoon sauce onto serving plates; top with chicken breasts.

Makes 4 servings

Spinach, Cheese and Prosciutto-Stuffed Chicken Breast

Chicken Marsala

1 tablespoon butter
2 boneless skinless chicken breasts, halved
1 cup sliced carrots
1 cup sliced fresh mushrooms
⅓ cup chicken broth
⅓ cup HOLLAND HOUSE® Marsala Cooking Wine

Melt butter in skillet over medium-high heat. Add chicken; cook 5 minutes. Turn chicken over; add remaining ingredients. Bring to a boil; simmer 15 to 20 minutes until juices run clear. Serve over cooked fettuccine, if desired.

Makes 4 servings

Cheesy Chicken Tetrazzini

2 whole chicken breasts, boned, skinned and cut into 1-inch pieces (about 1½ pounds)
2 tablespoons butter or margarine
1½ cups sliced mushrooms
1 small red pepper, cut into julienne strips
½ cup sliced green onions
¼ cup all-purpose flour
1¾ cups chicken broth
1 cup light cream or half-and-half
2 tablespoons dry sherry
½ teaspoon salt
¼ teaspoon black pepper
¼ teaspoon dried thyme leaves, crushed
1 package (8 ounces) tri-color rotelle pasta, cooked until just tender and drained
¼ cup freshly grated Parmesan cheese
2 tablespoons chopped fresh parsley
1 cup shredded JARLSBERG Cheese

In skillet, brown chicken in butter. Add mushrooms and brown. Add red pepper and green onions; cook several minutes, stirring occasionally. Stir in flour and cook several minutes until blended. Gradually blend in chicken broth, cream and sherry. Cook, stirring, until thickened and smooth. Season with salt, pepper and thyme. Toss sauce with pasta, Parmesan cheese and parsley. Spoon into 1½-quart baking dish. Bake at 350°F for 30 minutes. Top with Jarlsberg cheese. Bake until cheese is melted.

Makes 6 servings

Simmered Tuscan Chicken

   2 tablespoons olive oil
   1 pound boneless, skinless chicken breasts, cut into 1-inch cubes
   2 cloves garlic, finely chopped
   2 medium potatoes, cut into ½-inch cubes (about 4 cups)
   1 medium red bell pepper, cut into large pieces
   1 jar (26 ounces) RAGÚ® Old World Style® Pasta Sauce
   1 teaspoon dried basil leaves, crushed
     Salt and ground black pepper to taste

In 12-inch skillet, heat olive oil over medium-high heat and cook chicken with garlic until chicken is thoroughly cooked. Remove chicken and set aside.

In same skillet, add potatoes and bell pepper. Cook over medium heat, stirring occasionally, 5 minutes. Stir in remaining ingredients. Bring to a boil over high heat. Reduce heat to low and simmer, covered, stirring occasionally 35 minutes or until potatoes are tender. Return chicken to skillet and heat through.   *Makes 6 servings*

BelGioioso® Gorgonzola Chicken

   6 skinless boneless chicken breast halves
   ¼ teaspoon salt
   ⅛ teaspoon pepper
   2 tablespoons butter
   1 tablespoon olive oil
   ½ cup chicken stock or broth
   ¼ cup whipping cream
   ¼ cup (2 ounces) creamy BELGIOIOSO® Gorgonzola Cheese
   ½ cup chopped walnuts (optional)
   2 tablespoons chopped fresh basil

Season chicken with salt and pepper. Pound chicken to ¼-inch thickness. Melt butter with olive oil over medium-high heat in large skillet. Add chicken and cook 2 to 3 minutes on each side or until chicken is cooked throughout. Remove to serving platter and cover.

Add stock to skillet and cook over high heat 1 minute. Reduce heat to low and gradually add cream, stirring constantly. Blend in BelGioioso Gorgonzola Cheese; stir until cheese is melted and sauce is smooth. Continue cooking until sauce is of desired consistency. Pour sauce over chicken and garnish with walnuts and basil. Serve with wild rice.   *Makes 6 servings*

Simmered Tuscan Chicken

Chicken Rustigo

4 boneless skinless chicken breast halves
2 tablespoons olive oil, divided
1 package (10 ounces) fresh mushrooms, sliced
¾ cup chicken broth
¼ cup dry red wine or water
3 tablespoons *French's*® Spicy Brown Mustard
2 plum tomatoes, coarsely chopped
1 can (14 ounces) artichoke hearts, drained and quartered
2 teaspoons cornstarch

1. Season chicken with salt and pepper. Heat *1 tablespoon oil* in large nonstick skillet over medium-high heat. Cook chicken 5 minutes or until browned on both sides. Remove and set aside.

2. Heat *1 tablespoon oil* in same skillet over medium-high heat until hot. Add mushrooms. Cook and stir 5 minutes or until mushrooms are tender. Stir in broth, wine and mustard. Return chicken to skillet. Add tomatoes and artichoke hearts. Heat to boiling. Reduce heat to medium-low. Cook, covered, 10 minutes or until chicken is no longer pink in center.

3. Combine cornstarch and *1 tablespoon cold water* in small bowl. Stir into skillet. Heat to boiling. Cook, stirring, over high heat about 1 minute or until sauce thickens. Serve with hot cooked orzo pasta, if desired.   *Makes 4 servings*

Prep Time: 10 minutes • Cook Time: 21 minutes

Cutlets Milanese

1 package (about 1 pound) PERDUE® FIT 'N EASY® Thin-Sliced Turkey Breast Cutlets or
   Chicken Breast
  Salt and black pepper to taste
1 egg beaten with 1 teaspoon water
½ cup Italian seasoned bread crumbs
½ cup grated Parmesan cheese
2 to 3 tablespoons olive oil

Season cutlets with salt and pepper. On waxed paper, combine bread crumbs and Parmesan cheese. Dip cutlets in egg mixture and roll in bread crumb mixture. In large nonstick skillet over medium-high heat, heat oil. Add cutlets and sauté 3 minutes per side until golden brown and no longer pink in center.   *Makes 4 servings*

Prep Time: 6 to 8 minutes • Cook Time: 6 minutes

Turkey Piccata

⅓ cup all-purpose flour
½ teaspoon salt
½ teaspoon black pepper
1 boneless turkey breast (1 pound), sliced into 4 slices
3 tablespoons olive oil, divided
1½ cups sliced fresh mushrooms
2 cloves garlic, crushed
½ cup chicken broth
2 tablespoons lemon juice
½ teaspoon dried oregano
3 tablespoons pine nuts
2 tablespoons chopped fresh parsley

1. Combine flour, salt and pepper in resealable food storage bag. Add turkey; shake to coat evenly.

2. Heat 2 tablespoons oil in large skillet over medium-high heat. Add turkey; cook 3 minutes on each side or until lightly browned and turkey is no longer pink in center. Remove from skillet to serving plate. Cover with foil and keep warm.

3. Add remaining 1 tablespoon oil to skillet. Heat over medium-high heat. Add mushrooms and garlic; cook and stir 2 minutes. Add broth, lemon juice and oregano; bring to a boil. Reduce heat to medium; simmer, uncovered, 3 minutes.

4. Spoon sauce mixture over turkey. Sprinkle with pine nuts and parsley. Serve immediately.

Makes 4 servings

Serving Suggestion: Serve with rice pilaf, sliced fresh tomatoes and garlic bread.

Prep and Cook Time: 20 minutes

Turkey Piccata

Chicken Florentine

    4 (6-ounce) skinless, boneless chicken breast halves
    ¼ teaspoon salt
    ¼ teaspoon freshly ground black pepper
    ½ cup Italian seasoned dry bread crumbs
    1 egg, separated
    1 (10 ounces) package frozen chopped spinach, thawed, well drained
    ⅛ teaspoon nutmeg
    2 tablespoons olive oil
    4 slices SARGENTO® Deli Style Sliced Mozzarella Cheese
    1 cup prepared tomato basil or marinara spaghetti sauce, heated

1. Sprinkle chicken with salt and pepper. Place bread crumbs in a shallow plate. Beat egg white in a shallow bowl. Dip each chicken breast in egg white, letting excess drip off; roll lightly in crumbs, patting to coat well. (At this point, chicken may be covered and refrigerated up to 4 hours before cooking.)

2. Combine spinach, egg yolk and nutmeg; mix well. Heat oil in a large skillet over medium-high heat until hot. Add chicken breasts; cook 3 minutes per side or until golden brown. Reduce heat to low. Top each chicken breast with ¼ of spinach mixture and 1 slice of cheese. Cover skillet and continue cooking 6 minutes or until chicken is no longer pink in center. Spoon spaghetti sauce over chicken.   *Makes 4 servings*

Chicken with Escarole and Eggplant

    4 bone-in chicken breast halves (about 1½ pounds)
    2 tablespoons olive oil
    1 tablespoon chopped garlic
    1 large head escarole, chopped
    1 small eggplant (about 1 pound), peeled and cubed
    1 jar (26 ounces) RAGÚ® Robusto!® Pasta Sauce

1. Preheat oven to 450°F. Season chicken, if desired, with salt and pepper. In bottom of broiler pan without rack, arrange chicken. Roast 40 minutes or until chicken is no longer pink.

2. Meanwhile, in 12-inch skillet, heat olive oil over medium heat and cook garlic, stirring occasionally, 30 seconds. Add escarole and eggplant and cook covered, stirring occasionally, 5 minutes, or until escarole is wilted. Stir in Ragú Pasta Sauce and cook 10 minutes or until vegetables are tender.

3. With slotted spoon, remove vegetables to large serving platter, then top with chicken. Serve, if desired, over hot cooked pasta or rice.   *Makes 4 servings*

Prep Time: 10 minutes • Cook Time: 40 minutes

Skillet Chicken Cacciatore

2 tablespoons olive or vegetable oil
1 cup sliced red onion
1 medium green bell pepper, cut into strips (about 1 cup)
2 cloves garlic, minced
1 pound (about 4) boneless, skinless chicken breast halves
1 can (14½ ounces) CONTADINA® Recipe Ready Diced Tomatoes with
    Italian Herbs, undrained
¼ cup dry white wine or chicken broth
½ teaspoon salt
¼ teaspoon ground black pepper
1 tablespoon chopped fresh basil *or* 1 teaspoon dried basil leaves, crushed

1. Heat oil in large skillet over medium-high heat. Add onion, bell pepper and garlic; sauté 1 minute.

2. Add chicken; cook 6 to 8 minutes or until chicken is no longer pink in center.

3. Add undrained tomatoes, wine, salt and black pepper. Simmer, uncovered, 5 minutes. Serve over hot cooked rice or pasta, if desired. Sprinkle with basil.   *Makes 6 servings*

Venetian Chicken with Creamy Pesto Sauce

1 tablespoon olive oil
1 red or yellow bell pepper, cut into chunks
1 pound boneless skinless chicken breasts or thighs, cut into 1-inch chunks
½ teaspoon salt
¼ teaspoon black pepper
½ cup half-and-half
½ cup prepared pesto sauce
3 cups hot cooked spaghetti or vermicelli pasta (6 ounces uncooked)
¼ cup grated Asiago or Parmesan cheese

1. Heat oil in large nonstick skillet over medium heat. Add bell pepper; cook and stir 3 minutes. Add chicken, salt and pepper; cook and stir 5 minutes.

2. Stir in half-and-half and pesto sauce; cook, stirring occasionally, about 3 minutes or until chicken is cooked through and bell pepper is tender (about 5 minutes for chicken thighs).

3. Serve over pasta; sprinkle with cheese.   *Makes 4 servings*

Skillet Chicken Cacciatore

Chicken Piccata

  3 tablespoons all-purpose flour
  ½ teaspoon salt
  ¼ teaspoon black pepper
  4 boneless skinless chicken breasts (4 ounces each)
  2 teaspoons olive oil
  1 teaspoon butter
  2 cloves garlic, minced
  ¾ cup reduced-sodium chicken broth
  1 tablespoon lemon juice
  2 tablespoons chopped Italian parsley
  1 tablespoon drained capers

1. Combine flour, salt and pepper in shallow plate. Reserve 1 tablespoon of flour mixture.

2. Place chicken between sheets of plastic wrap. Using flat side of meat mallet or rolling pin, pound chicken to ½-inch thickness. Coat chicken in flour mixture, shaking off excess.

3. Heat oil and butter in large nonstick skillet over medium heat until butter is melted. Cook chicken 4 to 5 minutes per side until no longer pink in center. Transfer to serving platter and cover loosely with foil.

4. Add garlic to same skillet; cook and stir over medium heat 1 minute. Add reserved flour mixture; cook and stir 1 minute. Add broth and lemon juice; cook 2 minutes, stirring frequently until sauce thickens. Stir in parsley and capers. Spoon sauce over chicken.   *Makes 4 servings*

After cooking chicken, some brown bits remain in the skillet. These bits will contribute a lot of flavor to the sauce, so prepare the sauce in this skillet. When you add the broth and lemon juice, whisk or stir the mixture, being sure to scrape up all the browned bits from the bottom of the skillet.

Chicken Piccata

Parmesan Turkey

   1 pound turkey breast or chicken breasts, cut into ⅛- to ¼-inch-thick slices
½ teaspoon salt
¼ teaspoon black pepper
   2 tablespoons butter, melted
   2 cloves garlic, minced
½ cup grated Parmesan cheese
   1 cup marinara sauce, warmed
   2 tablespoons chopped fresh basil

1. Preheat broiler. Sprinkle turkey slices with salt and pepper. Place turkey in single layer in 15×10×1-inch jelly-roll pan.

2. Combine butter and garlic in small bowl; brush over turkey. Broil turkey 4 to 5 inches from heat source 2 minutes; turn. Sprinkle with cheese. Broil 2 to 3 minutes more or until turkey is no longer pink in center. Transfer to serving plates. To serve, spoon sauce over turkey; sprinkle with basil.

Makes 4 servings

Variation: Preheat oven to 350°F. Sprinkle turkey with salt and pepper. Brown turkey on both sides in 1 to 2 tablespoons hot oil in medium skillet. Place browned turkey in small casserole dish or 9-inch square baking pan. Top with pasta sauce; cover dish with foil. Bake 30 minutes or until turkey is no longer pink in center. Remove from oven. Sprinkle with Parmesan cheese and basil.

Chicken Pomodoro

   2 cloves garlic, finely minced
   4 boneless, skinless chicken breast halves
⅛ teaspoon crushed red pepper flakes (optional)
   1 tablespoon olive oil
   1 can (14½ ounces) DEL MONTE® Stewed Tomatoes - Italian Recipe
   2 small zucchini, cut in half lengthwise and sliced crosswise
   2 tablespoons thinly sliced fresh basil leaves *or* ½ teaspoon dried basil
⅓ cup whipping cream

1. Rub garlic over chicken. Sprinkle with red pepper flakes. Season with salt and pepper, if desired.

2. Brown chicken in oil in large skillet over medium-high heat. Stir in tomatoes, zucchini and basil.

3. Cook, uncovered, over medium-high heat 15 minutes or until sauce is thickened and chicken is no longer pink, stirring occasionally.

4. Stir in cream; heat through. *Do not boil.*

Makes 4 servings

Prep Time: 8 minutes • Cook Time: 23 minutes

Pollo alla Firènze

2 cups plus 2 tablespoons dry sherry, divided
6 boneless skinless chicken breasts
3 tablespoons olive oil
3 cups shredded spinach leaves
2 cups coarsely chopped mushrooms
1 cup grated carrots
⅓ cup sliced green onions
2 cloves garlic, minced
Salt and black pepper
1½ cups Italian salad dressing
1 cup seasoned dry bread crumbs
⅓ cup grated Romano cheese

1. Pour 2 cups sherry into large, shallow dish. Add chicken, turning to coat. Cover; marinate in refrigerator 3 hours.

2. To prepare filling, heat oil in large skillet over medium heat. Add spinach, mushrooms, carrots, green onions, garlic and remaining 2 tablespoons sherry. Cook and stir 3 to 5 minutes or until spinach is completely wilted; season to taste with salt and pepper. Set aside to cool.

3. Place dressing in shallow bowl; set aside. Combine bread crumbs and cheese in another shallow bowl; set aside.

4. Preheat oven to 375°F. Grease 13×9-inch baking pan; set aside.

5. Remove chicken from marinade; discard marinade. Cut pocket horizontally into side of each chicken breast. Fill pockets with spinach mixture. Secure pockets with toothpicks to enclose filling.

6. Coat each filled chicken breast with dressing, shaking off excess. Coat each chicken breast with bread crumb mixture.

7. Place chicken in single layer in prepared baking pan. Drizzle with remaining dressing. Cover; bake 15 minutes. Uncover; bake 10 minutes or until chicken is no longer pink in center. Remove toothpicks before serving.

Makes 6 servings

Chicken Puttanesca-Style

2 tablespoons olive oil
1 (2½- to 3-pound) chicken, cut into pieces
1 medium onion, sliced
¼ cup balsamic vinegar
1 jar (26 ounces) RAGÚ® Old World Style® Pasta Sauce
1 cup pitted ripe olives
1 tablespoon drained capers

In 12-inch skillet, heat olive oil over medium-high heat and brown chicken. Remove chicken and set aside; drain.

In same skillet, add onion and vinegar and cook over medium heat, stirring occasionally, 3 minutes. Stir in Ragú Old World Style Pasta Sauce. Return chicken to skillet and simmer, covered, 25 minutes or until chicken is thoroughly cooked. Stir in olives and capers; heat through. Serve, if desired, over hot cooked rice and garnish with chopped fresh parsley. *Makes 4 servings*

Chicken Puttanesca-Style

Fish and Shellfish

page 154

page 158

page 162

Italy, surrounded by the Adriatic Sea on the east and the Mediterranean Sea on the west, is famous for its seafood dishes. Every region with a seacoast has creative and delicious ways to prepare fish and shellfish. From clams, shrimp and squid to swordfish, snapper and tuna, you'll discover why seafood has a special place on Italian menus.

Grilled Swordfish Sicilian Style

pictured on page 145

2 to 3 tablespoons extra-virgin olive oil
1 clove garlic, minced
4 teaspoons lemon juice
½ teaspoon salt
   Black pepper
2 tablespoons capers, drained
1 tablespoon chopped fresh oregano or basil
1½ pounds swordfish steaks (¾ inch thick)
   Lemon slices (optional)

1. Prepare grill for direct cooking.

2. Heat olive oil in small saucepan over low heat; add garlic. Cook 1 minute. Remove from heat; cool slightly. Whisk in lemon juice, salt and pepper until salt is dissolved. Stir in capers and oregano; set aside.

3. Place swordfish on oiled grid over medium heat. Grill 7 to 8 minutes, turning once, or until fish just begins to flake when tested with fork. Serve fish with lemon juice mixture. Garnish with lemon slices.

Makes 4 to 6 servings

Note: Instead of marinating the raw swordfish steaks, this recipe calls for grilling the swordfish, then serving it with a marinade for a delicious fresh flavor.

To prevent fish from sticking to the grill grid, brush the cold grid with vegetable oil or spray it with nonstick cooking spray.

Baked Snapper with Artichokes

Juice of 2 lemons, divided
3 large artichokes
8 tablespoons extra-virgin olive oil, divided
2 cloves garlic, minced
1 dressed red snapper or sea bass (about 2 pounds) with head and tail intact
Salt and black pepper
3 small sprigs fresh rosemary, divided
1 tablespoon finely chopped fresh parsley

1. Pour half the lemon juice and squeezed lemon halves in large bowl. Fill bowl half full with cold water; set aside. Reserve remaining lemon juice.

2. To prepare artichokes, bend back dark outer leaves and snap off at base. Continue snapping off leaves until bottom halves are yellow. Cut 1½ inches off tops of artichokes; trim stems to 1 inch. Peel tough green layer from stem and base. Cut artichokes lengthwise (from tops) into quarters; place quarters in lemon water to help prevent discoloration.

3. Working with 1 artichoke quarter at a time, remove small heart-shaped leaves from center by grasping with fingers, then pulling and twisting. Scoop out fuzzy choke with spoon. Cut artichoke quarters lengthwise into thin slices. Return slices to lemon water. Repeat with remaining artichoke quarters.

4. Drain artichoke slices. Heat 6 tablespoons oil in large skillet over medium heat. Add artichokes and garlic. Cover; cook 5 minutes until tender, stirring occasionally.

5. Preheat oven to 425°F. Rinse fish; pat dry with paper towels. Season fish inside and out with salt and pepper. Place in baking pan.

6. Stuff fish cavity with 1 sprig rosemary and as many artichoke slices as will fit. Arrange remaining artichoke slices and 2 sprigs rosemary around fish.

7. Combine reserved lemon juice, remaining 2 tablespoons oil and parsley; drizzle over fish. Bake 30 minutes or until fish just begins to flake when tested with fork, basting occasionally with pan juices.

Makes 4 servings

Red Snapper Scampi

¼ cup (½ stick) butter, softened
1 tablespoon dry white wine
1½ teaspoons minced garlic
½ teaspoon grated lemon peel
⅛ teaspoon black pepper
1½ pounds red snapper, orange roughy or grouper fillets (about 4 to 5 ounces each)

1. Preheat oven to 450°F. Combine butter, wine, garlic, lemon peel and pepper in small bowl.

2. Place fish in foil-lined shallow baking pan. Top with seasoned butter. Bake 10 to 12 minutes or until fish just begins to flake when tested with fork. *Makes 4 servings*

Tip: Serve fish with mixed salad greens, if desired. Or add sliced carrots, zucchini and bell pepper cut into matchstick-size strips to the baking pan for an easy vegetable side dish.

Prep and Cook Time: 12 minutes

Tuna and Pasta Frittata

1 tablespoon olive oil
2 cups cooked spaghetti
4 eggs
¼ cup prepared pesto sauce
2 tablespoons milk
1 (3-ounce) STARKIST Flavor Fresh Pouch® Tuna (Albacore or Chunk Light)
½ cup shredded mozzarella cheese

Preheat broiler. In medium ovenproof skillet, heat oil over medium-high heat; sauté spaghetti. In bowl, combine eggs, pesto sauce and milk; blend well. Add tuna; pour mixture over hot spaghetti. Cook over medium-low heat, stirring occasionally until eggs are almost completely set. Sprinkle cheese over cooked eggs; place under broiler until cheese is bubbly and golden. Serve hot or at room temperature. *Makes 2 to 4 servings*

Prep Time: 8 minutes

Red Snapper Scampi

Primavera Sauce with Artichokes and Shrimp

2 tablespoons olive oil
1 cup diced carrots
1 cup diced celery
1 small onion, diced
3 cloves garlic, finely chopped
1 can (28 ounces) CONTADINA® Recipe Ready Crushed Tomatoes with Italian Herbs
½ teaspoon salt
¼ teaspoon ground black pepper
8 ounces medium raw shrimp, peeled and deveined
1 cup sliced artichoke hearts, drained
Fresh chopped basil (optional)

1. Heat oil in large skillet over high heat. Add carrots, celery, onion and garlic. Cook for 4 to 5 minutes or until carrots are crisp-tender.

2. Add crushed tomatoes, salt and pepper. Bring to boil. Add shrimp and artichoke hearts. Cook for 2 to 3 minutes or until shrimp turn pink.

3. Reduce heat to low; simmer for 2 minutes to blend flavors. Sprinkle with basil. Serve over hot cooked pasta or rice, if desired. *Makes 6 servings*

Prep Time: 12 minutes • Cook Time: 12 minutes

Primavera Sauce with Artichokes and Shrimp

Swordfish Pomodoro

1½ pounds swordfish steaks (¾ inch thick)
¼ teaspoon plus ⅛ teaspoon salt, divided
⅛ teaspoon black pepper
2 tablespoons all-purpose flour
2 teaspoons olive oil
1 medium onion, halved and cut into thin slices
1 clove garlic, minced
1½ cups chopped seeded tomatoes
⅓ cup drained mild giardiniera*
2 tablespoons dry white wine (optional)
1 tablespoon chopped fresh oregano *or* 1 teaspoon dried oregano
2 tablespoons canola oil

Giardiniera is an Italian term for pickled vegetables. Available mild or hot, you can find giardiniera in the pickle or ethnic foods section of the grocery store.

1. Sprinkle fish with ⅛ teaspoon salt and pepper. Dredge fish in flour, shaking off excess; set aside.

2. Heat olive oil in large skillet over medium heat. Add onion; cook and stir 4 minutes or until tender. Add garlic; cook and stir 30 seconds. Add tomatoes; cook 3 minutes, stirring occasionally. Stir in giardiniera, wine, if desired, oregano and remaining ¼ teaspoon salt. Cook about 3 minutes or until most liquid is evaporated.

3. Meanwhile, heat canola oil in 12-inch nonstick skillet over medium-high heat. Cook fish 4 minutes; turn and cook 3 to 4 minutes or until fish just begins to flake when tested with fork. Serve tomato mixture over fish. *Makes 4 to 6 servings*

Prep Time: 10 minutes • **Cook Time:** 20 minutes

The secret to cooking fish successfully is to avoid overcooking it which will result in a dry texture. Cook fish only until it has lost its translucent appearance and the juices are milky white in color.

Fish and Shellfish • 153

Tuna Steaks with Tomatoes & Olives

- 2 teaspoons olive oil
- 1 small onion, quartered and sliced
- 1 clove garlic, minced
- 1⅓ cups chopped tomatoes
- ¼ cup sliced drained ripe olives
- 2 anchovy fillets, finely chopped (optional)
- 2 tablespoons chopped fresh basil
- ¼ teaspoon salt, divided
- ⅛ teaspoon red pepper flakes
- 4 tuna steaks (¾ inch thick)
- Black pepper
- Nonstick cooking spray
- ¼ cup toasted pine nuts (optional)

1. Heat oil in large skillet over medium heat. Add onion; cook and stir 4 minutes. Add garlic; cook and stir about 30 seconds. Add tomatoes; cook 3 minutes, stirring occasionally. Stir in olives, anchovy fillets, if desired, basil, ⅛ teaspoon salt and red pepper flakes. Cook until most liquid is evaporated.

2. Meanwhile, sprinkle tuna with remaining ⅛ teaspoon salt and black pepper. Spray large nonstick skillet with cooking spray. Heat over medium-high heat. Cook tuna 2 minutes on each side or until medium-rare. Serve with tomato mixture. Garnish with pine nuts.

Makes 4 servings

Tuna Steak with Tomatoes & Olives

Squid Mediterranean

  2 pounds cleaned whole squid (body and tentacles)
  1 tablespoon olive oil
¾ cup finely chopped onion
  1 clove garlic, minced
  2 (16-ounce) cans Italian-style tomatoes, drained and chopped
  3 tablespoons sliced black olives
  1 tablespoon capers
½ teaspoon dried oregano
¼ teaspoon dried marjoram
⅛ teaspoon crushed red pepper

Cut body of squid into ½-inch slices; set aside. Heat olive oil in a large skillet; add onion and garlic. Cook until onion is tender. Add squid and remaining ingredients. Bring to a boil. Cover, reduce heat and simmer 30 minutes or until squid is tender. *Makes 4 servings*

Prep Time: about 45 minutes

Favorite recipe from **National Fisheries Institute**

Swordfish Messina Style

  2 tablespoons olive or vegetable oil
½ cup chopped fresh parsley
  2 tablespoons chopped fresh basil *or* 2 teaspoons dried basil leaves, crushed
  2 cloves garlic, minced
  1 can (8 ounces) CONTADINA® Tomato Sauce
¾ cup sliced fresh mushrooms
  1 tablespoon capers
  1 tablespoon lemon juice
⅛ teaspoon ground black pepper
  3 pounds swordfish or halibut steaks

1. Heat oil in small saucepan. Add parsley, basil and garlic; sauté for 1 minute. Reduce heat to low. Add tomato sauce, mushrooms and capers; simmer, uncovered, for 5 minutes.

2. Stir in lemon juice and pepper. Place swordfish in single layer in greased 13×9-inch baking dish; cover with sauce.

3. Bake in preheated 400°F oven for 20 minutes or just until fish flakes when tested with fork.
Makes 8 servings

Prep Time: 5 minutes • **Cook Time:** 26 minutes

Shrimp Scampi

⅓ cup clarified butter*
¼ cup minced garlic
1½ pounds large shrimp, peeled and deveined
6 green onions, thinly sliced
¼ cup dry white wine
2 tablespoons lemon juice
8 sprigs fresh parsley, finely chopped
Salt and black pepper
Lemon slices and additional fresh parsley sprigs (optional)

*To clarify butter, melt butter over low heat. Skim off the white foam that forms on top, then strain clear golden butter through cheesecloth. Discard milky residue at the bottom of pan. Clarified butter will keep, covered, in the refrigerator for up to 2 months.

1. Heat butter in large skillet over medium heat. Add garlic; cook and stir 1 to 2 minutes or until soft but not brown. Add shrimp, onions, wine and lemon juice; cook 2 to 4 minutes or until shrimp turn pink and opaque, stirring occasionally. *Do not overcook.*

2. Add chopped parsley; season with salt and pepper. Garnish with lemon slices and parsley sprigs.
Makes 4 servings

Nutty Pan-Fried Trout

2 tablespoons olive oil
4 trout fillets (about 6 ounces each)
½ cup seasoned dry bread crumbs
½ cup pine nuts

1. Heat oil in large skillet over medium heat. Lightly coat fish with bread crumbs. Add to skillet.

2. Cook 4 minutes on each side or until fish just begins to flake when tested with fork. Transfer fish to serving platter; keep warm.

3. Add pine nuts to drippings in skillet. Cook and stir 3 minutes or until nuts are lightly toasted. Sprinkle over fish.
Makes 4 servings

Shrimp Scampi

Grilled Sea Bass with Ripe Olive 'n' Caper Salsa

1 cup sliced California Ripe Olives
½ cup seeded, diced Roma tomatoes
½ cup chopped oil-packed sun-dried tomatoes
¼ cup minced red onion
¼ cup chopped fresh basil
3 tablespoons capers
2 tablespoons chopped fresh parsley
2 tablespoons balsamic-style vinaigrette dressing
1 teaspoon minced garlic
8 (6-ounce) sea bass or other white fish fillets
Olive oil

Preheat grill or broiler. Combine all ingredients except sea bass and olive oil in large bowl. Mix well. Adjust seasoning with salt and pepper. Cover and chill. Brush both sides of fillets with olive oil and season with salt and pepper. Grill or broil until fish is firm to the touch, about 5 minutes on each side. Serve each fillet with about ¼ cup of Ripe Olive 'n' Caper Salsa. *Makes 8 servings*

Favorite recipe from *California Olive Industry*

Grilled Sea Bass with Ripe Olive 'n' Caper Salsa

Elegant Crabmeat Frittata

3 tablespoons butter or margarine, divided
½ cup (about 4 ounces) sliced mushrooms
2 green onions, thinly sliced
8 eggs, separated
¼ cup milk
½ teaspoon hot pepper sauce
¼ teaspoon salt
½ pound lump crabmeat, flaked, shells and cartilage removed
½ cup (2 ounces) shredded Swiss cheese

1. Melt 2 tablespoons butter in large ovenproof skillet over medium-high heat. Add mushrooms and onions; cook and stir 3 to 5 minutes or until vegetables are tender. Remove from skillet; set aside.

2. Beat egg yolks in medium bowl with electric mixer at high speed until slightly thickened and lemon colored. Stir in milk, hot pepper sauce and salt.

3. Beat egg whites in clean large bowl with electric mixer at high speed until foamy. Gradually add to egg yolk mixture, gently whisking just until blended.

4. Melt remaining 1 tablespoon butter in skillet over low heat; pour in egg mixture. Cook until egg mixture is almost set. Remove from heat.

5. Preheat broiler. Broil frittata 4 to 6 inches from heat until top is set. Top with crabmeat, mushroom mixture and cheese. Return frittata to broiler; broil until cheese is melted. Garnish as desired. Serve immediately.

Makes 4 servings

Choose a heavy skillet with a sloping side and ovenproof handle to prepare this frittata. Low heat will help to keep the frittata moist.

Salads and Vegetables

page 170

page 174

page 180

Vegetables have always been an important part of Italian cuisine. Italian cooks have found creative and flavorful ways to prepare them. Try any of these recipes that feature favorite Italian vegetables like eggplant, tomatoes, zucchini, peppers and spinach, and you'll soon learn how fabulous salads and vegetable dishes can be.

Broccoli Italian Style

pictured on page 165

    1¼ pounds broccoli
    2 tablespoons lemon juice
    1 teaspoon extra-virgin olive oil
    1 clove garlic, minced
    1 teaspoon chopped fresh parsley
      Dash black pepper

1. Trim broccoli, discarding tough stems. Cut broccoli into florets with 2-inch stems. Peel remaining broccoli stems; cut into ½-inch-thick slices.

2. Bring 1 quart water to a boil in large saucepan over high heat. Add broccoli; return to a boil. Reduce heat to medium-high. Cook, uncovered, 3 to 5 minutes or until broccoli is fork-tender. Drain; arrange evenly in serving dish.

3. Combine lemon juice, oil, garlic, parsley and pepper in small bowl. Pour over broccoli; toss to coat. Let stand, covered, 1 to 2 hours before serving to allow flavors to blend.   *Makes 4 servings*

Tomato, Prosciutto & Fresh Mozzarella Salad

    1 package (10 ounces) DOLE® Organic Salad Blend Spring Mix with Herbs or
        Baby Lettuces Salad
    1 cup yellow and red pear or cherry tomatoes, halved
 1½ ounces prosciutto, chopped *or* 5 strips bacon, cooked, drained and crumbled
    4 ounces fresh mozzarella cheese, drained and cut into bits or regular mozzarella cheese, cut
        into julienne strips
    1 cup sliced red onion
    1 cup croutons
    ¼ cup prepared balsamic vinaigrette dressing

• Combine salad blend, tomatoes, prosciutto, cheese, onion and croutons in large bowl.

• Pour vinaigrette over salad; toss to evenly coat.   *Makes 4 servings*

Prep Time: 20 minutes

Classica™ Fontina Potato Surprise

2½ **pounds potatoes**
3 **tablespoons butter or margarine, melted**
¼ **cup CLASSICA™ Grated Parmesan cheese**
1 **egg**
1 **egg white**
⅛ **teaspoon salt**
⅛ **teaspoon ground nutmeg**
4 **tablespoons fine dry bread crumbs, divided**
8 **ounces fontina, cut into chunks**
¼ **cup freshly grated sharp provolone cheese**
¼ **pound GALBANI® Prosciutto di Parma, cut into small pieces**
2 **tablespoons butter or margarine, cut into small pieces**

In large saucepan, cook potatoes in boiling water over medium-low heat until tender; drain. Cool slightly; peel and cut in half. Press potatoes through food mill or mash until smooth. Combine potatoes, melted butter, Classica™ Grated Parmesan cheese, egg, egg white, salt and nutmeg in large bowl; mix until smooth. Set aside.

Sprinkle half of bread crumbs in well-buttered 9-inch round baking dish. Tilt dish to coat. Spread about half of potato mixture on bottom and side of dish.

Combine fontina, provolone and Galbani® Prosciutto di Parma in small bowl. Sprinkle over potato mixture in dish.

Cover with remaining potato mixture; sprinkle with remaining bread crumbs. Dot with pieces of butter.

Bake in preheated 350°F oven 40 minutes or until thin crust forms. Let stand 5 minutes.

Invert baking dish onto serving plate, tapping gently to remove. Serve immediately.

Makes about 8 servings

Fontina is a traditional Italian cheese made from cow's milk. It has a mild nutty flavor. Since it melts easily, fontina is perfect for many uses.

Tomato-Fresh Mozzarella Salad

   Vinaigrette Dressing (recipe follows)
1 pound fresh mozzarella
1 pound ripe tomatoes
   Fresh basil leaves
   Salt and black pepper

Prepare Vinaigrette Dressing. Cut mozzarella into ¼-inch slices. Cut tomatoes into ¼-inch slices. Arrange mozzarella slices, tomato slices and basil leaves overlapping on plate. Drizzle with dressing. Sprinkle with salt and pepper. *Makes 4 servings*

Vinaigrette Dressing

1 tablespoon balsamic vinegar or red wine vinegar
¼ teaspoon Dijon mustard
   Pinch *each* of salt, black pepper and sugar
¼ cup extra-virgin olive oil

Whisk together vinegar, mustard, salt, pepper and sugar in small bowl until smooth. Add oil in thin stream, whisking until mixture is smooth. Refrigerate until ready to use. Whisk again before serving. *Makes about ½ cup*

Sautéed Swiss Chard

1 large bunch Swiss chard or kale (about 1 pound)
1 tablespoon olive oil
3 cloves garlic, minced
¾ teaspoon salt
¼ teaspoon black pepper
1 tablespoon balsamic vinegar (optional)
¼ cup pine nuts, toasted

1. Rinse chard in cold water; shake off excess water but do not dry. Finely chop stems and coarsely chop leaves.

2. Heat oil in large saucepan or Dutch oven over medium heat. Add garlic; cook and stir 2 minutes. Add chard, salt and pepper. Cover and steam for 2 minutes or until chard begins to wilt. Uncover; turn with tongs and cook about 5 minutes or until chard is evenly wilted.

3. Stir in vinegar, if desired; sprinkle with pine nuts before serving. *Makes 4 servings*

Tomato-Fresh Mozzarella Salad

Peperonata

   2 tablespoons extra-virgin olive oil
   4 large red, yellow or orange bell peppers, cut into thin strips
   2 cloves garlic, coarsely chopped
  12 pimiento-stuffed green olives or pitted black olives, whole, sliced or chopped
   2 to 3 tablespoons white wine vinegar or red wine vinegar
  ¼ teaspoon salt
  ¼ teaspoon black pepper

1. Heat olive oil in 12-inch skillet over medium-high heat. Add bell peppers; cook 8 to 9 minutes or until edges of peppers begin to brown, stirring frequently.

2. Reduce heat to medium. Add garlic; cook and stir 1 to 2 minutes. *Do not allow garlic to brown.* Add olives, vinegar, salt and black pepper. Cook 1 to 2 minutes or until all liquid is evaporated.

Makes 4 to 5 servings

Note: Traditionally, peperonata is served hot as a condiment with meat dishes. Or, it can be chilled and served as part of an antipasti selection. It also makes a great side dish which complements both chicken and pork.

Gnocchi with BelGioioso® Gorgonzola

   2 pounds potatoes
  2⅓ cups all-purpose flour
   1 egg
     Salt to taste
   1 cup BELGIOIOSO® Gorgonzola
   1 tablespoon water
     Black pepper to taste

Boil and peel potatoes; mash. Add flour, egg and salt; mix by hand until dough is soft and compact. With floured hands, make small potato rolls (almost like dumplings). Drop into boiling water to cook. Meanwhile, cut BelGioioso Gorgonzola into cubes; melt in pan over low heat. Add water and pepper. Toss cooked gnocchi with Gorgonzola sauce; serve.

Makes 6 servings

Italian Bread Salad

1 loaf (about 12 ounces) hearty peasant-style bread (such as sourdough, rosemary-olive oil or roasted garlic)
1 medium red onion, sliced
1 teaspoon minced garlic
⅓ cup balsamic and olive oil vinaigrette
1½ cups halved grape tomatoes or cherry tomatoes
⅓ cup pitted oil- or salt-cured black and green olives
1 package European salad mix or pre-washed baby spinach
Grated Parmesan cheese
Black pepper

1. Preheat oven to 250°F. Tear bread into large pieces. Place on baking sheet. Bake 10 to 15 minutes or until slightly dry but not browned. Set aside to cool.

2. Place onion and garlic in large salad bowl. Add vinaigrette and stir to coat. Set aside 5 minutes to allow flavors to blend.

3. Add tomatoes and olives; stir gently to coat with dressing. Add greens, bread cubes and cheese; toss gently. Add more vinaigrette if needed and season to taste with pepper.

Makes 4 servings

Tip: You can use day-old bread that has started to dry out for this recipe. Bread that is a little too hard or stale can be softened by sprinkling it with water.

Italian Bread Salad

No Frying Eggplant Parmesan

    2 cups seasoned dry bread crumbs
1½ cups grated Parmesan cheese, divided
    2 medium eggplants (about 2 pounds), peeled and cut into ¼-inch slices
    4 eggs, beaten with 3 tablespoons water
    1 jar (26 ounces) RAGÚ® ROBUSTO!® Pasta Sauce
1½ cups shredded mozzarella cheese (about 6 ounces)

Preheat oven to 350°F. In medium bowl, combine bread crumbs and ½ cup Parmesan cheese. Dip eggplant slices in egg mixture, then bread crumb mixture. On lightly oiled baking sheets, arrange eggplant slices in single layer. Bake 25 minutes or until eggplant is golden.

In 13×9-inch baking dish, evenly spread 1 cup Pasta Sauce. Layer ½ of baked eggplant slices, then 1 cup sauce and ½ cup Parmesan cheese; repeat layers. Cover with aluminum foil and bake 45 minutes. Remove foil and sprinkle with mozzarella cheese. Bake uncovered an additional 10 minutes or until cheese is melted. *Makes 6 servings*

Prep Time: 10 minutes • **Cook Time:** 1 hour, 20 minutes

Fra Diavolo Antipasto Salad

    1 cup prepared Italian salad dressing
    3 to 4 tablespoons *Frank's® RedHot®* Original Cayenne Pepper Sauce or to taste
¼ cup chopped fresh Italian parsley
    6 cups assorted vegetables, such as cauliflower, carrots, tomatoes, celery, zucchini and/or
        mushrooms, cut into bite-size pieces
    1 jar (6 ounces) Tuscan peppers, drained
¼ pound mild provolone cheese, cut into small sticks
¼ pound fresh mozzarella cheese, cut into small cubes*
¼ pound hard salami, cut into small cubes
    Romaine lettuce leaves

*Look for fresh mozzarella in the deli section of your supermarket.

Whisk together salad dressing, *Frank's RedHot* Sauce and parsley in small bowl. Place vegetables, peppers, cheeses and salami in large bowl. Add dressing; toss well to coat evenly. Cover and marinate in refrigerator 1 hour. Arrange lettuce on large platter. Spoon salad over lettuce just before serving. *Makes 6 appetizer servings*

Prep Time: 20 minutes • **Marinate Time:** 1 hour

Italian Artichoke and Rotini Salad

  4 ounces uncooked whole wheat or tri-colored rotini pasta
  1 can (14 ounces) quartered artichoke hearts, drained
  4 ounces (½ cup) sliced pimientos
  1 can (2½ ounces) sliced black olives, drained
  2 tablespoons finely chopped onion
  2 teaspoons dried basil
  ½ clove garlic, minced
  ⅛ teaspoon black pepper
  3 tablespoons cider vinegar
  1 tablespoon extra-virgin olive oil
  ¼ teaspoon salt

1. Cook rotini according to package directions. Meanwhile, combine artichokes, pimientos, olives, onion, basil, garlic and pepper in medium bowl.

2. Drain pasta; rinse under cold running water to cool completely. Drain well. Add pasta to artichoke mixture; toss to blend. Just before serving, combine vinegar, oil and salt; whisk until well blended. Toss with pasta mixture to coat.   *Makes 6 servings*

Fennel with Black Olive Dressing

  1¼ pounds (about 2 medium-size heads) fennel
  ⅓ cup lemon juice
  ¼ cup olive or salad oil
  ⅔ cup pitted California ripe olives, coarsely chopped
     Salt and pepper

Trim stems and root ends from fennel; core. Reserve feathery wisps of fennel for garnish, if desired. Slice fennel crosswise into ¼-inch-thick pieces. In 4- to 5-quart pan, bring 3 to 4 quarts water to a boil over high heat. Add fennel and cook, uncovered, just until tender, about 5 minutes. Drain; immerse fennel in ice water until cold. Drain well again. In small bowl, whisk lemon juice and oil; stir in olives and add salt and pepper to taste. To serve, divide fennel among 6 salad plates and spoon dressing over fennel. Garnish with reserved feathery wisps of fennel, if desired.

Makes 6 servings

Prep Time: 10 minutes • **Cook Time:** About 5 minutes

Favorite recipe from *California Olive Industry*

Potato Gnocchi with Tomato Sauce

  2 pounds baking potatoes (3 or 4 large)
     Tomato Sauce (recipe follows) or prepared meatless pasta sauce
⅔ to 1 cup all-purpose flour, divided
  1 egg yolk
½ teaspoon salt
⅛ teaspoon ground nutmeg (optional)
     Freshly grated Parmesan cheese

1. Preheat oven to 425°F. Pierce potatoes several times with fork. Bake 1 hour or until soft. Meanwhile, prepare Tomato Sauce; set aside.

2. Cut baked potatoes in half lengthwise; cool slightly. Scoop pulp from skins with spoon into medium bowl; discard skins. Mash potatoes until smooth. Add ⅓ cup flour, egg yolk, salt and nutmeg, if desired, to potato pulp; mix well to form dough.

3. Turn out dough onto well-floured surface. Knead in enough remaining flour to form smooth dough that is not sticky. Divide dough into 4 equal portions. Roll each portion with hands on lightly floured surface into ¾- to 1-inch-wide rope. Cut each rope into 1-inch pieces; gently press thumb into center of each piece to make indentation. Space gnocchi slightly apart on lightly floured kitchen towel to prevent them from sticking together.

4. Bring 4 quarts salted water to a gentle boil in Dutch oven over high heat. To test gnocchi cooking time, drop several into water; cook 1 minute or until they float to surface. Remove from water with slotted spoon and taste for doneness. (If gnocchi start to dissolve, shorten cooking time by several seconds.) Cook remaining gnocchi in batches, removing with slotted spoon to warm serving dish.

5. Serve immediately topped with warm Tomato Sauce; sprinkle with cheese.

Makes 4 servings

Tomato Sauce

  2 tablespoons olive oil or butter
  1 clove garlic, minced
  2 pounds ripe plum tomatoes, peeled, seeded and chopped
  1 teaspoon sugar
¼ cup finely chopped prosciutto or cooked ham (optional)
  1 tablespoon finely chopped fresh basil
     Salt and black pepper

Heat oil in medium saucepan over medium heat. Add garlic; cook 30 seconds or until fragrant. Stir in tomatoes and sugar. Cook 10 minutes or until most of liquid is evaporated. Stir in prosciutto, if desired, and basil. Cook 2 minutes. Season to taste with salt and pepper.　*Makes about 2 cups*

Potato Gnocchi with Tomato Sauce

Italian Vegetable Stew

1 teaspoon olive oil
2 medium zucchini, halved lengthwise and thinly sliced
1 medium eggplant, chopped
1 large onion, thinly sliced
⅛ teaspoon ground black pepper
1 jar (26 ounces) RAGÚ® Light Pasta Sauce
3 tablespoons grated Parmesan cheese
1 box (10 ounces) couscous

1. In 12-inch nonstick skillet, heat olive oil over medium heat and cook zucchini, eggplant, onion and pepper, stirring occasionally, 15 minutes or until vegetables are golden.

2. Stir in Ragú Pasta Sauce and cheese. Bring to a boil over high heat. Reduce heat to low and simmer covered 10 minutes.

3. Meanwhile, prepare couscous according to package directions. Serve vegetable mixture over hot couscous. *Makes 4 servings*

Polenta with Sautéed Mushrooms

⅔ cup yellow cornmeal
1 cup milk
1 cup reduced-sodium chicken broth
½ teaspoon plus ⅛ teaspoon salt, divided
1 tablespoon olive oil
2 (4-ounce) packages sliced mixed exotic mushrooms *or* 8 ounces cremini mushrooms, sliced
3 cloves garlic, minced
1 teaspoon dried thyme
¼ teaspoon black pepper
¼ cup port wine or beef broth
½ cup grated Parmesan cheese, divided

1. Whisk together cornmeal, milk, broth and ½ teaspoon salt in medium saucepan. Bring to a boil over high heat. Reduce heat to medium-low; simmer 10 minutes or until thickened, whisking occasionally.

2. Meanwhile, heat oil in large skillet over medium heat. Add mushrooms, garlic, thyme, pepper and remaining ⅛ teaspoon salt; cook and stir 6 minutes. Add port; simmer 4 minutes or until liquid is reduced and mushrooms are tender.

3. Stir ¼ cup cheese into polenta. Transfer to serving plates; top with mushroom mixture and remaining ¼ cup cheese. *Makes 4 servings*

Italian Vegetable Stew

Artichoke Frittata

1 can (14 ounces) artichoke hearts, drained
3 teaspoons extra-virgin olive oil, divided
½ cup minced green onions
5 eggs
½ cup (2 ounces) shredded Swiss cheese
2 tablespoons grated Parmesan cheese
1 tablespoon minced fresh parsley
1 teaspoon salt
¼ teaspoon black pepper

1. Chop artichoke hearts; set aside.

2. Heat 2 teaspoons oil in large skillet over medium heat. Add green onions; cook and stir until tender. Remove from skillet.

3. Beat eggs in medium bowl until light. Stir in artichokes, green onions, cheeses, parsley, salt and pepper.

4. Heat remaining 1 teaspoon oil in same skillet over medium heat. Pour egg mixture into skillet. Cook 4 to 5 minutes or until bottom is lightly browned. Place large plate over skillet; invert frittata onto plate. Return frittata, uncooked side down, to skillet. Cook about 4 minutes more or until center is set. Cut into wedges. *Makes 6 to 8 servings*

Sicilian-Style Pasta Salad

1 pound dry rotini pasta
2 cans (14½ ounces each) CONTADINA® Recipe Ready Diced Tomatoes with Italian Herbs, undrained
1 cup sliced yellow bell pepper
1 cup sliced zucchini
8 ounces cooked bay shrimp
1 can (2¼ ounces) sliced pitted ripe olives, drained
2 tablespoons balsamic vinegar

1. Cook pasta according to package directions; drain.

2. Combine pasta, undrained tomatoes, bell pepper, zucchini, shrimp, olives and vinegar in large bowl; toss well.

3. Cover. Chill before serving. *Makes 10 servings*

Artichoke Frittata

Panzanella

4 ounces day-old French bread, cubed*
4 plum tomatoes, chopped
3 tablespoons extra-virgin olive oil
2 tablespoons red wine vinegar
1 clove garlic, minced
½ teaspoon salt
¼ cup chopped fresh basil

You can substitute day-old whole wheat bread, sourdough bread or pita bread for the Italian bread. Simply cube it or tear it into small pieces.

1. Combine bread cubes and tomatoes in medium serving bowl.

2. Whisk together oil, vinegar, garlic and salt in small bowl; stir in basil. Pour over bread mixture; toss until well mixed.   *Makes 6 servings*

Prep Time: 10 minutes

Fennel with Parmesan Bread Crumbs

2 large fennel bulbs
½ cup dry bread crumbs
¼ cup lemon juice
1 tablespoon grated Parmesan cheese
1 tablespoon capers
2 teaspoons olive oil
⅛ teaspoon black pepper
½ cup reduced-sodium chicken broth
    Minced fennel tops and red bell pepper (optional)

1. Preheat oven to 375°F. Spray 9-inch square baking dish with nonstick cooking spray; set aside.

2. Remove outer leaves and wide base from fennel bulbs. Slice bulbs crosswise.

3. Combine fennel and ¼ cup water in medium nonstick skillet with tight-fitting lid. Bring to a boil over high heat; reduce heat to medium. Cover and steam 4 minutes or until fennel is crisp-tender. Cool slightly; arrange in prepared baking pan.

4. Combine bread crumbs, lemon juice, Parmesan cheese, capers, oil and black pepper in small bowl. Sprinkle bread crumb mixture over fennel; pour broth over top.

5. Bake, uncovered, 20 to 25 minutes or until golden brown. Garnish with fennel tops and bell pepper.   *Makes 4 servings*

Panzanella

Tuscan Vegetable Stew

2 tablespoons olive oil

2 teaspoons minced garlic

2 packages (4 ounces each) sliced mixed exotic mushrooms *or* 1 package (8 ounces) sliced button mushrooms

¼ cup sliced shallots or chopped sweet onion

1 jar (7 ounces) roasted red peppers

1 can (14½ ounces) Italian-style stewed tomatoes, undrained and chopped

1 can (19 ounces) cannellini beans, rinsed and drained

1 bunch fresh basil*

1 tablespoon balsamic vinegar

Salt and black pepper

Grated Romano, Parmesan or Asiago cheese

If fresh basil is not available, add 2 teaspoons dried basil to stew with tomatoes.

1. Heat oil and garlic in large deep skillet over medium heat. Add mushrooms and shallots; cook and stir 5 minutes.

2. Meanwhile, drain and rinse peppers; cut into 1-inch pieces. Add beans, tomatoes and peppers to skillet; bring to a boil. Reduce heat to medium-low. Cover and simmer 10 minutes, stirring once.

3. Cut basil leaves crosswise into thin strips to measure ¼ cup. Stir basil and vinegar into stew; add salt and black pepper to taste. Sprinkle each serving with cheese.   *Makes 4 servings*

Prep and Cook Time: 18 minutes

Chopping canned tomatoes can be messy. Instead, try snipping them in the can with kitchen scissors.

Marinated Vegetable Salad

- 3 tablespoons plus 1½ teaspoons white wine vinegar
- 2 tablespoons minced fresh basil *or* ½ teaspoon dried basil
- ½ teaspoon salt
- ⅛ teaspoon black pepper
- ⅛ teaspoon sugar
- 6 tablespoons extra-virgin olive oil
- 2 ripe medium tomatoes
- ⅓ cup pitted green olives
- ⅓ cup Italian- or Greek-style black olives
- 1 head green or red leaf lettuce
- 1 small head curly endive
- 2 heads Belgian endive

1. To prepare dressing, place vinegar, basil, salt, pepper and sugar in blender or food processor. With motor running, add oil in slow steady stream until thoroughly blended.

2. Cut tomatoes into wedges. Combine tomatoes and olives in medium bowl. Add dressing; toss lightly. Cover and let stand at room temperature 30 minutes to blend flavors, stirring occasionally.

3. Rinse leaf lettuce and curly endive; drain well. Refrigerate greens until ready to assemble salad. Core Belgian endive and separate leaves; rinse and drain well.

4. To serve, layer leaf lettuce, curly endive and Belgian endive leaves in large, shallow serving bowl.

5. Remove tomatoes and olives from dressing with slotted spoon and place on top of greens. Spoon remaining dressing over salad. Serve immediately or cover and refrigerate up to 30 minutes.

Makes 6 servings

Marinated Vegetable Salad

Eggplant Italiano

 2 tablespoons olive oil, divided
 2 medium onions, thinly sliced
 2 stalks celery, cut into 1-inch pieces
 1¼ pounds eggplant, cut into 1-inch cubes
 1 can (about 14 ounces) diced tomatoes, drained
 ½ cup pitted ripe olives, cut crosswise in half
 2 tablespoons balsamic vinegar
 1 tablespoon sugar
 1 tablespoon drained capers
 1 teaspoon dried oregano or basil
  Salt and black pepper to taste

1. Heat wok or large skillet over medium-high heat 1 minute or until hot. Add 1 tablespoon oil to wok; heat 30 seconds. Add onions and celery; cook and stir about 2 minutes or until tender. Move onions and celery up side of wok. Reduce heat to medium.

2. Add remaining 1 tablespoon oil to wok; heat 30 seconds. Add eggplant; cook and stir about 4 minutes or until tender. Add tomatoes; mix well. Cover; cook 10 minutes.

3. Stir olives, vinegar, sugar, capers and oregano into eggplant mixture. Season with salt and pepper.   *Makes 6 servings*

Rigatoni with Broccoli

 8 ounces uncooked rigatoni pasta
 1 bunch fresh broccoli, trimmed and separated into florets with 1-inch stems
 1 tablespoon FILIPPO BERIO® Extra Virgin Olive Oil
 1 clove garlic, minced
  Crushed red pepper
  Grated Parmesan cheese

Cook pasta according to package directions until al dente (tender but still firm). Add broccoli during last 5 minutes of cooking time; cook until broccoli is tender-crisp. Drain pasta and broccoli; transfer to large bowl. Meanwhile, in small skillet, heat olive oil over medium heat until hot. Add garlic; cook and stir 1 to 2 minutes or until golden. Pour oil mixture over hot pasta mixture; toss until lightly coated. Season to taste with red pepper. Top with cheese.   *Makes 4 servings*

Eggplant Italiano

Marinated Antipasto Pasta Salad

Antipasto Dressing
  2 cloves garlic
  ⅔ cup balsamic vinegar or white wine vinegar
  2 tablespoons Dijon mustard
  1 teaspoon salt
  ½ teaspoon sugar
  1 cup extra-virgin olive oil

Pasta Salad
  4 ounces uncooked ziti or mostaccioli pasta
  6 ounces Genoa salami or summer sausage, diced
  6 ounces provolone, smoked mozzarella or regular mozzarella cheese, diced
  12 kalamata olives
  12 red and/or yellow cherry tomatoes
  4 peperoncini peppers, sliced and seeded
    Lettuce leaves
    Chopped fresh basil

1. To prepare dressing, drop garlic through feed tube of food processor while motor is running. Process until garlic is minced. Add vinegar, mustard, salt and sugar; process until blended. With motor running, slowly pour oil through feed tube; process until thickened. Cover; refrigerate 2 hours or up to 1 month.

2. Cook pasta according to package directions; drain and rinse with cool water. Drain well.

3. Combine pasta, salami, cheese, olives, tomatoes and peperoncini in medium bowl. Add dressing; toss to coat. Cover; refrigerate 2 hours or up to 2 days. Serve on lettuce leaves. Sprinkle with basil.   *Makes 6 servings*

Serving Suggestion: Serve with crusty Italian bread or crisp bread sticks.

Pizza and Panini

page 202

page 200

page 206

Bread is one of Italy's most revered foods. It is served simply with olive oil and as the foundation for bruschetta, pizza and panini. This chapter offers a fantastic selection of pizza and panini recipes so you can share these popular Italian-inspired treats with your family. You are sure to get rave reviews every time you serve them.

Pizza with Caramelized Onions and Ripe Olives

pictured on page 195

Pizza Dough (recipe follows)
1 tablespoon **cornmeal**
¼ cup **FILIPPO BERIO® Extra-Virgin or Pure Olive Oil plus some for the pan**
2 large **onions, sliced**
¼ teaspoon **salt**
¼ teaspoon **dried oregano**
½ cup **dry-cured ripe olives, pitted**

Prepare the Pizza Dough. Coat a 14 or 15-inch round pizza pan with oil. Sprinkle with the cornmeal; set aside. Punch down the dough and place on a lightly floured work surface to sit for 5 minutes. With lightly floured hands or rolling pin, pat or roll dough into a 15 or 16-inch circle. Transfer to the prepared pan. Fold the edges to make a rounded border. Cover with plastic wrap and set aside for about 15 minutes or until slightly risen.

Preheat the oven to 450°F. Place a large sauté pan over high heat. Add the oil and heat. Add the onions. Stir. Cover the pan and cook for 2 to 3 minutes or until the onions start to brown. Stir. Reduce the heat to medium.

Cook, stirring occasionally, for about 10 minutes or until onions are browned. Add the salt and oregano. Spread the onions over the prepared crust. Sprinkle with the olives. Bake for about 15 minutes or until the crust is golden. Remove to a cooling rack for 5 minutes.

Note: One pound of thawed frozen commercial bread dough may replace the pizza dough recipe.

Pizza Dough

1¼ cups **warm water (105°F to 115°F)**
1 envelope (¼ ounce) **active dry yeast**
1 tablespoon **FILIPPO BERIO® Extra-Virgin or Pure Olive Oil**
3 to 3½ cups **flour**
½ teaspoon **salt**

Coat a large bowl with oil; set aside. Mix the water and the yeast in another large bowl. Add the oil and 1 cup flour. Beat until smooth. Add 1 cup flour and the salt; beat until smooth. Add 1 cup flour. Stir until the mixture forms a ball. Place the remaining ½ cup flour on a work surface. Push most of the flour to the side. With a dough scraper, lift the dough onto the surface. Sprinkle lightly with flour. With the scraper, fold the dough several times to get rid of surface stickiness. With your hands, knead for 5 to 6 minutes until the dough is resilient. Use additional flour only to prevent surface sticking. Some flour may remain. Place in the prepared bowl. Coat lightly with oil. Cover with plastic wrap. Set aside to rise for about 45 minutes, or until doubled in size. Punch down the dough. Shape into a ball and transfer to a work surface. Let sit 5 minutes. Shape, add toppings, and bake according to recipe directions. To prepare in a food processor: In the bowl of a food processor fitted with a plastic or metal blade, process the ingredients according to recipe directions.

Makes one 15-inch round pizza crust, or 6 calzoni

Note: To freeze the unbaked pizza crust, roll or pat the dough according to recipe directions. Place on pizza pan dusted with cornmeal. Cover tightly with plastic wrap, then wrap in aluminum foil. Store in the freezer for up to 1 month. To bake, remove from the freezer (no need to thaw). Remove wrappings. Top and bake according to recipe directions.

Caramelized Onion Focaccia

2 tablespoons plus 1 teaspoon olive oil, divided
4 medium onions, cut in half and thinly sliced
½ teaspoon salt
2 tablespoons water
1 tablespoon chopped fresh rosemary
¼ teaspoon ground black pepper
1 loaf (16 ounces) frozen bread dough, thawed
1 cup (4 ounces) shredded fontina cheese
¼ cup grated Parmesan cheese

1. Heat 2 tablespoons oil in large skillet over high heat. Add onions and salt; cook about 10 minutes or until onions begin to brown, stirring occasionally. Stir in water. Reduce heat to medium; partially cover and cook about 20 minutes or until onions are deep golden brown, stirring occasionally. Remove from heat; stir in rosemary and pepper. Let cool slightly.

2. Meanwhile, brush 13×9-inch baking pan with remaining 1 teaspoon oil. Roll out dough to 13×9-inch rectangle on lightly floured surface. Transfer dough to prepared pan; cover and let rise in warm, draft-free place 30 minutes.

3. Preheat oven to 375°F. Prick dough all over (about 12 times) with fork. Sprinkle fontina cheese over dough; top with caramelized onions. Sprinkle with Parmesan cheese.

4. Bake 18 to 20 minutes or until golden brown. Remove from pan to wire rack. Cut into pieces. Serve warm.

Makes about 2 dozen pieces

Mozzarella, Pesto and Fresh Tomato Panini

- 8 slices country Italian, sourdough or other firm-textured bread
- 8 slices SARGENTO® Deli Style Sliced Mozzarella Cheese
- ⅓ cup prepared pesto
- 4 large slices ripe tomato
- 2 tablespoons olive oil

1. Top each of 4 slices of bread with 1 slice of cheese. Spread pesto over cheese. Top with tomatoes and remaining slices of cheese. Close sandwiches with remaining 4 slices of bread.

2. Brush olive oil lightly over both sides of sandwiches. Cook sandwiches over medium-low coals or in preheated ridged grill pan over medium heat 3 to 4 minutes per side or until bread is toasted and cheese is melted.   *Makes 4 servings*

Prep Time: 5 minutes • Cook Time: 8 minutes

Tuna Pizza with Caponata and Prosciutto

- 1 package (16 ounces) Italian bread shell for pizza
- 2 teaspoons olive oil
- 1 can (7½ ounces) caponata
- 1 (3-ounce) STARKIST Flavor Fresh Pouch® Tuna (Albacore)
- 8 slices (1 ounce) prosciutto
- 2 to 3 plum tomatoes, sliced ¼ inch thick
- 1 cup crumbled feta cheese
- 1 cup shredded mozzarella cheese
- Crushed red pepper (optional)

Place bread shell on foil-lined baking sheet; brush to edge with oil. Spread caponata to within 1 inch of edge. Top with tuna, prosciutto, tomatoes, feta and mozzarella cheeses. Bake in 450°F oven 10 to 12 minutes or until cheeses are melted and pizza is heated through. Cool 1 minute before slicing. Serve with crushed red pepper, if desired.   *Makes 4 servings*

Prep Time: 20 minutes

Mozzarella, Pesto and Fresh Tomato Panini

Caramelized Onion and Olive Pizza

          2 tablespoons olive oil
    1½ pounds onions, thinly sliced
          2 teaspoons fresh rosemary *or* 1 teaspoon dried rosemary
    ¼ cup water
          1 tablespoon balsamic vinegar
          1 cup California ripe olives, sliced
          1 (12-inch) prebaked thick pizza crust
          2 cups (8 ounces) shredded mozzarella cheese

Heat oil in medium nonstick skillet until hot. Add onions and rosemary. Cook, stirring frequently, until onions begin to brown and browned bits begin to stick to bottom of skillet, about 15 minutes. Stir in ¼ cup water; scrape up any browned bits. Reduce heat to medium-low and continue to cook, stirring occasionally, until onions are golden and sweet-tasting, 15 to 30 minutes longer; add more water, 1 tablespoon at a time, if onion mixture appears dry. Remove pan from heat and stir in vinegar, scraping up any browned bits from pan. Gently stir in olives. Place crust on pizza pan or baking sheet. Spoon onion mixture into center of crust. Sprinkle with cheese. Bake in 450°F oven until cheese is melted and just beginning to brown, about 15 minutes. Cut into wedges and serve warm.   *Makes 8 to 10 servings*

Prep Time: 15 minutes • **Cook Time:** about 1 hour

Favorite recipe from ***California Olive Industry***

When caramelizing onions, the goal is to cook them slowly until they are golden brown in color and have developed a sweet flavor. Watch them carefully, lowering the heat if the onions begin to brown too quickly.

Caramelized Onion and Olive Pizza

Pizza Sandwich

    1 loaf (12 ounces) focaccia
  ½ cup prepared pizza sauce
  20 slices pepperoni
    8 slices (1 ounce each) mozzarella cheese
    1 can (2¼ ounces) sliced mushrooms, drained
       Red pepper flakes (optional)
       Olive oil

1. Cut focaccia horizontally in half. Spread cut sides of both halves with pizza sauce. Layer bottom half with pepperoni, cheese and mushrooms; sprinkle with red pepper flakes, if desired. Cover sandwich with top of focaccia. Brush outside of sandwich lightly with olive oil.

2. Heat large nonstick skillet over medium heat. Add sandwich; press down with spatula or weigh down with small plate. Cook sandwich 4 to 5 minutes per side or until cheese melts and sandwich is golden brown. Cut into wedges to serve.   *Makes 4 to 6 servings*

Panini with Prosciutto, Mozzarella and Ripe Olives

    1 cup California ripe olives, sliced
  ¼ cup chopped fresh basil
    8 wedges prepared herb focaccia
  ⅓ cup coarse mustard
    1 pound prosciutto, sliced
  24 ounces mozzarella, thinly sliced
    4 cups arugula, washed, dried

Combine sliced olives and basil in bowl. Mix well and reserve. Slice each focaccia wedge horizontally in half. Spread cut sides of each wedge with 1 teaspoon mustard. Layer bottom halves with 2 tablespoons olive mixture, 2 ounces prosciutto, 3 ounces mozzarella and ½ cup arugula. Top with remaining focaccia halves.   *Makes 8 servings*

Favorite recipe from *California Olive Industry*

Three-Pepper Pizza

    1 cup (½ of 15 ounce can) CONTADINA® Four Cheese Pizza Sauce
    1 (12-inch) prepared pre-baked pizza crust
  1½ cups (6 ounces) shredded mozzarella cheese, divided
    ½ each: red, green and yellow bell peppers, sliced into thin rings
    2 tablespoons shredded Parmesan cheese
    1 tablespoon chopped fresh basil *or* 1 teaspoon dried basil leaves, crushed

1. Spread pizza sauce onto crust to within 1 inch of edge.

2. Sprinkle with 1 cup mozzarella cheese, bell peppers, remaining mozzarella cheese and Parmesan cheese.

3. Bake according to pizza crust package directions or until crust is crisp and cheese is melted. Sprinkle with basil.   *Makes 8 servings*

Grilled Italian Chicken Panini

    6 small portobello mushroom caps (about 6 ounces)
    ½ cup plus 2 tablespoons balsamic vinaigrette dressing
    1 loaf (16 ounces) Italian bread, cut into 12 slices
  12 slices provolone cheese
  1½ cups chopped cooked chicken
    1 jar (12 ounces) roasted red peppers, drained

1. Brush mushroom caps with 2 tablespoons dressing. Cook 5 to 7 minutes over medium-high heat in nonstick skillet until soft. Cut each mushroom cap diagonally into ½-inch slices. Set aside.

2. To assemble sandwiches, layer 6 bread halves evenly in following order: 1 cheese slice, ¼ cup chicken, 1 sliced mushroom cap, one-sixth roasted red peppers and another cheese slice. Top with remaining bread slices. Brush both sides of each sandwich with remaining dressing.

3. Preheat grill pan and panini press* at medium heat 5 minutes. Grill sandwiches 4 to 6 minutes until cheese is melted and bread is golden, turning once during cooking.   *Makes 6 sandwiches*

*If you don't have a grill pan and panini press, grill sandwiches in a nonstick skillet. Place a clean heavy pan on top of sandwiches to weigh them down during grilling.

Tip: A rotisserie chicken will yield just enough chicken for this recipe.

Portobello & Fontina Sandwiches

    2 teaspoons olive oil
    2 large portobello mushrooms, stems removed
      Salt and black pepper
    2 to 3 tablespoons sun-dried tomato pesto
    4 slices crusty Italian bread
    4 ounces fontina cheese, sliced
    ½ cup fresh basil leaves

1. Preheat broiler. Line baking sheet with foil.

2. Drizzle oil over both sides of mushrooms; season with salt and pepper. Place mushrooms, gill sides up, on prepared baking sheet. Broil mushrooms about 4 minutes per side or until tender. Cut into ¼-inch-thick slices.

3. Spread pesto evenly on 2 bread slices; layer with mushrooms, cheese and basil. Top with remaining bread slices. Brush outsides of sandwiches lightly with oil.

4. Place large grill pan or skillet over medium heat until hot. Add sandwiches; press down with spatula or weigh down with small plate. Cook sandwiches 4 to 5 minutes per side or until cheese melts and sandwiches are golden brown. *Makes 2 sandwiches*

BelGioioso® Caprese Sandwiches

    1 long (about 24 inches) slender baguette
    1 clove garlic, cut in half
    2 medium, fully-ripened tomatoes, thinly sliced and slices cut in half
  24 fresh basil leaves
    8 ounces BELGIOIOSO® Fresh Mozzarella, cut into ½-inch cubes
    2 to 3 teaspoons extra-virgin olive oil
      Salt and freshly ground black pepper to taste

Make lengthwise cut down middle of baguette, starting on top of loaf and cut into, but not through, bottom. Gently open to make V-shaped cavity.

Rub cut sides of bread with garlic. Arrange tomato slices down each side of cavity followed by basil leaves.

In medium bowl, gently mix BelGioioso Fresh Mozzarella, oil, salt and pepper. Spoon mixture into loaf between rows of tomato and basil. Cut sandwich crosswise into 6-inch lengths. *Makes 4 sandwiches*

Portobello & Fontina Sandwich

Mozzarella-Prosciutto Panini

1 **BAYS® English Muffin, split**
½ **teaspoon bottled Italian dressing**
¼ **ounce prosciutto**
Thinly sliced Roma tomato
1½ **ounces smoked mozzarella, sliced to fit inside of muffin**
1 **teaspoon softened butter**

Preheat a heavy skillet or griddle over low heat until a spatter of water disappears quickly. Sprinkle inside of each muffin half with Italian dressing. Layer prosciutto, tomato and smoked mozzarella on bottom of muffin. Replace top. Spread softened butter on outside of sandwich.

Place sandwich bottom side down in preheated skillet. Place a heavy saucepan weighted with 2 cans or brick wrapped in heavy duty foil on top to flatten panini. Cook 3 minutes. Turn and cook on second side 3 minutes with weight in place until cheese starts to sizzle into pan. Remove weight and finish cooking.
Makes 1 serving

Turkey Cheddar Panini: For each panini, spread inside of bottom half of muffin with 2 teaspoons chutney; top with ½ ounce sliced turkey or cooked roast pork and 1 ounce Cheddar cheese. Spread 1 teaspoon softened butter on outside of sandwich. Cook 3 minutes per side as directed above.

Fontina-Caponata Panini: For each panini, spread inside of bottom half of muffin with 1 rounded tablespoonful of prepared caponata (eggplant appetizer); top with 1½ ounces Fontina or smoked mozzarella sliced to fit muffin. Spread 1 teaspoon softened butter on outside of sandwich. Cook as directed above.

Mozzarella-Prosciutto Panini

Spinach & Roasted Pepper Panini

1 loaf (12 ounces) onion focaccia
1½ cups spinach leaves (about 12 leaves)
1 jar (about 7 ounces) roasted red peppers, drained
4 ounces fontina cheese, thinly sliced
¾ cup thinly sliced red onion
Olive oil

1. Place focaccia on cutting board; cut in half horizontally. Layer bottom half with spinach, peppers, cheese and onion. Cover sandwich with top of bread. Brush outside of sandwich very lightly with olive oil. Cut sandwich into 4 equal pieces.

2. Heat large nonstick skillet over medium heat. Add sandwiches; press down lightly with spatula or weigh down with small plate. Cook sandwiches 4 to 5 minutes per side or until cheese melts and sandwiches are golden brown.   *Makes 4 servings*

Note: Focaccia can be found in the bakery section of most supermarkets. It is often available in different flavors, such as tomato, herb, cheese or onion. If you prefer to bake focaccia, you'll find a delightful recipe for Caramelized Onion Focaccia on page 197.

Spinach & Roasted Pepper Panini

Quattro Formaggio Pizza

1 (12-inch) Italian bread shell
½ cup prepared pizza or marinara sauce
4 ounces shaved or thinly sliced provolone cheese
1 cup (4 ounces) shredded smoked or regular mozzarella cheese
2 ounces Asiago or brick cheese, thinly sliced
¼ cup grated Parmesan or Romano cheese

1. Preheat oven to 450°F. Place bread shell on baking sheet; spread evenly with pizza sauce.

2. Top sauce with cheeses. Bake 14 minutes or until bread shell is golden brown and cheeses are melted. Cut into wedges; serve immediately. *Makes 4 servings*

Serving Suggestion: Serve with a tossed green salad.

Prep and Cook Time: 26 minutes

Broiled Gorgonzola Chicken Sandwiches

4 boneless skinless chicken breast halves
    Salt and black pepper
½ cup crumbled BELGIOIOSO® Gorgonzola Cheese
8 slices sourdough bread
    Lettuce leaves
1 teaspoon dried parsley

Preheat broiler. Rinse chicken; pat dry. Place chicken on unheated rack of broiler pan. Season with salt and pepper. Broil 4 to 5 inches from heat source 5 minutes; turn and brush with remaining 1 tablespoon Italian dressing. Broil 4 to 6 minutes or until chicken is tender and no longer pink. Sprinkle BelGioioso Gorgonzola Cheese evenly over chicken; return to broiler just until cheese melts. Line bread slices with lettuce; top with chicken. Sprinkle with parsley. *Makes 4 servings*

Quattro Formaggio Pizza

Sweet Endings

page 222

page 226

page 228

Italians usually serve fresh fruit or cheese as an ending for everyday dinners, saving richer treats for special occasions. Try some of the recipes from this exciting collection of both simple and elaborate sweets. Tiramisù, cappuccino, cannoli, biscotti, panettone and granita—there's a perfect Italian dessert for every occasion.

Cannoli Pastries

pictured on page 215

    18 to 20 Cannoli Pastry Shells* (recipe follows)
    4 cups (32 ounces) ricotta cheese
    1½ cups sifted powdered sugar
    2 teaspoons ground cinnamon
    ¼ cup diced candied orange peel, minced
    1 teaspoon grated lemon peel
    Additional powdered sugar
    2 squares (1 ounce each) semisweet chocolate, finely chopped

*You may substitute purchased cannoli shells. They can be found at Italian bakeries and delis or in the ethnic foods section of large supermarkets.

1. Prepare Cannoli Pastry Shells; set aside.

2. For cannoli filling, beat cheese in large bowl with electric mixer at medium speed until smooth. Add 1½ cups powdered sugar and cinnamon; beat at high speed 3 minutes. Add candied orange peel and lemon peel to cheese mixture; mix well. Cover and refrigerate until ready to serve.

3. To assemble, spoon cheese filling into pastry bag fitted with large plain tip. Pipe about ¼ cup filling into each cannoli pastry shell.* Dust Cannoli Pastries with additional powdered sugar to coat. Dip ends of pastries into chocolate. Arrange pastries on serving plate.

Makes 18 to 20 pastries

*Do not fill Cannoli Pastry Shells ahead of time or shells will become soggy.

Cannoli Pastry Shells

    1¾ cups all-purpose flour
    2 tablespoons sugar
    1 teaspoon grated lemon peel
    2 tablespoons cold butter
    1 egg
    6 tablespoons sweet marsala wine
    Vegetable oil

1. Combine flour, sugar and lemon peel in medium bowl; cut in butter with 2 knives or pastry blender until mixture resembles fine crumbs. Beat egg and marsala in small bowl; add to flour mixture. Stir with fork to form ball. Divide dough in half; shape into two 1-inch-thick square pieces. Wrap in plastic wrap and refrigerate at least 1 hour.

2. Heat 1½ inches oil in large saucepan to 325°F. Working with 1 piece of dough at a time, roll out on lightly floured surface to ¹⁄₁₆-inch thickness. Cut dough into 9 or 10 (4×3-inch) rectangles.

3. Wrap each rectangle around greased metal cannoli form or uncooked cannelloni pasta shell. Brush one edge of dough lightly with water; overlap with opposite edge and press firmly to seal.

4. Fry 2 or 3 cannoli shells at a time, 1 to 1½ minutes or until light brown, turning once. Remove with tongs; drain on paper towels.

5. Set aside until cool enough to handle. Carefully remove pastries from cannoli forms or pasta shells; cool completely. Repeat with remaining dough.   *Makes 18 to 20 pastry shells*

Orange Almond Fig Cake

   10 dried figs
2½ cups plus 2 tablespoons all-purpose flour, divided
   ½ cup ground almonds
1½ teaspoons baking powder
   ½ teaspoon ground cinnamon
   ¼ teaspoon salt
1¼ cups sugar
   ½ cup FILIPPO BERIO® Olive Oil
   2 eggs
   ½ cup fresh orange juice
      Finely grated peel of 1 orange
   ⅓ cup sliced almonds

Preheat oven to 350°F. Grease 10-inch tube pan with olive oil.

Remove stems from figs; cut figs into eighths. In small bowl, toss figs with 2 tablespoons flour.

In medium bowl, combine remaining 2½ cups flour, ground almonds, baking powder, cinnamon and salt.

In large bowl, beat sugar, olive oil and eggs with electric mixer at medium speed 2 to 3 minutes or until thick and creamy. Add flour mixture alternately with orange juice, mixing until blended. Add figs and orange peel; stir just until blended. Pour batter into prepared pan; sprinkle with sliced almonds.

Bake 50 to 60 minutes or until toothpick inserted into center comes out clean. Cool on wire rack 15 minutes. Remove from pan. Cool completely.   *Makes 12 servings*

Florentine Cookies

¼ cup (½ stick) unsalted butter
¼ cup sugar
1 tablespoon whipping cream
¼ cup sliced blanched almonds, finely chopped
¼ cup walnuts, finely chopped
5 red candied cherries, finely chopped
1 tablespoon golden or dark raisins, finely chopped
1 tablespoon crystallized ginger, finely chopped
1 tablespoon diced candied lemon peel, finely chopped
3 tablespoons all-purpose flour
4 squares (1 ounce each) semisweet chocolate, chopped

1. Preheat oven to 350°F. Grease 2 baking sheets.

2. Combine butter, sugar and cream in small heavy saucepan. Cook, uncovered, over medium heat until sugar dissolves and mixture boils, stirring constantly. Cook and stir 1 minute more; remove from heat. Stir in nuts, fruit, ginger and lemon peel. Add flour; mix well.

3. Spoon heaping teaspoonfuls batter onto prepared baking sheets, placing 4 cookies on each to allow room for spreading.

4. Bake cookies, 1 sheet at a time, 8 to 10 minutes or until deep brown. Remove baking sheet from oven to wire rack. (If cookies have spread unevenly, push in edges with metal spatula to round out shape.) Cool cookies 1 minute or until firm enough to remove from sheet; then quickly and carefully remove cookies to wire racks. Cool completely.

5. Melt chocolate in top of double boiler over hot, not boiling, water, stirring frequently; immediately remove top of double boiler from water. Let chocolate cool slightly.

6. Line baking sheets with waxed paper. Spread chocolate on bottoms of cookies. Place cookies, chocolate side up, on prepared baking sheets; let stand until chocolate is almost set. Score chocolate in zig-zag pattern with tines of fork. Let stand until completely set or refrigerate until firm. Store in airtight container in refrigerator. *Makes about 2 dozen cookies*

Note: Florentine cookies are believed to have been created in Austria, but this version showcases Italian dessert ingredients.

Quick Tiramisù

1 package (18 ounces) NESTLÉ® TOLL HOUSE® Refrigerated Mini Sugar Cookie Bar Dough
1 package (8 ounces) ⅓ less fat cream cheese
½ cup granulated sugar
¾ teaspoon TASTER'S CHOICE® 100% Pure Instant Coffee dissolved in ¾ cup cold water, *divided*
1 container (8 ounces) frozen whipped topping, thawed
1 tablespoon NESTLÉ® TOLL HOUSE® Baking Cocoa

PREHEAT oven to 325°F.

DIVIDE cookie dough into 20 pieces. Shape into 2½×1-inch oblong shapes. Place on ungreased baking sheets.

BAKE for 10 to 12 minutes or until light golden brown around edges. Cool on baking sheets for 1 minute; remove to wire racks to cool completely.

BEAT cream cheese and sugar in large mixer bowl until smooth. Beat in *¼ cup* Taster's Choice. Fold in whipped topping. Layer 6 cookies in 8-inch-square baking dish. Sprinkle each cookie with *1 teaspoon* Taster's Choice. Spread *one-third* cream cheese mixture over cookies. Repeat layers 2 more times with *12* cookies, *remaining* coffee and *remaining* cream cheese mixture. Cover; refrigerate for 2 to 3 hours. Crumble *remaining* cookies over top. Sift cocoa over cookies. Cut into squares. *Makes 6 to 8 servings*

Creamy Cappuccino Brownies

1 package (21 to 24 ounces) brownie mix, plus ingredients to prepare mix
1 tablespoon coffee crystals *or* 1 teaspoon espresso powder
2 tablespoons warm water
1 cup (8 ounces) Wisconsin Mascarpone cheese
3 tablespoons granulated sugar
1 egg
   Powdered sugar

Grease bottom of 13×9-inch baking pan. Prepare brownie mix according to package directions. Pour half of batter into prepared pan. In medium bowl, dissolve coffee crystals in warm water; add Mascarpone, granulated sugar and egg. Blend until smooth. Drop by spoonfuls over brownie batter; top with remaining brownie batter. With knife, swirl cheese mixture through brownies creating marbled effect. Bake at 375°F 30 to 35 minutes or until toothpick inserted in center comes out clean. Sprinkle with powdered sugar. *Makes 2 dozen brownies*

Favorite recipe from **Wisconsin Milk Marketing Board**

Classic Anise Biscotti

¾ cup (about 4 ounces) whole blanched almonds
2¼ cups all-purpose flour
1 teaspoon baking powder
¾ teaspoon salt
¾ cup sugar
½ cup unsalted butter, softened
3 eggs
2 tablespoons brandy
2 teaspoons grated lemon peel
1 tablespoon anise seeds

1. Preheat oven to 375°F. To toast almonds, spread on baking sheet. Bake 6 to 8 minutes or until light brown; turn off oven. Let almonds cool slightly; coarsely chop.

2. Combine flour, baking powder and salt in small bowl. Beat sugar and butter in medium bowl with electric mixer at medium speed until light and fluffy. Add eggs, 1 at a time, beating well after each addition. Stir in brandy and lemon peel. Add flour mixture gradually; stir until smooth. Stir in chopped almonds and anise seeds. Cover and refrigerate dough 1 hour or until firm.

3. Preheat oven to 375°F. Grease 2 baking sheets. Divide dough in half. Shape half of dough into 12×2-inch log on lightly floured surface. (Dough will be fairly soft.) Pat smooth with lightly floured fingertips. Transfer to prepared baking sheet. Repeat with remaining half of dough to form second log. Bake 20 to 25 minutes or until logs are light golden brown. Cool slightly on baking sheet on wire rack. *Reduce oven temperature to 350°F.*

4. Cut logs diagonally with serrated knife into ½-inch-thick slices. Place slices flat in single layer on ungreased baking sheets.

5. Bake 8 minutes. Turn slices; bake 10 to 12 minutes or until cookies are light brown and dry. Remove cookies to wire racks; cool completely. Store cookies in airtight container up to 2 weeks.

Makes about 4 dozen cookies

Chocolate Hazelnut Torte

1 cup hazelnuts, toasted and skins removed*
¾ cup sugar, divided
¼ cup I CAN'T BELIEVE IT'S NOT BUTTER!® Spread
12 squares (1 ounce each) semi-sweet chocolate, divided
6 eggs, at room temperature
¼ cup brewed espresso coffee or coffee liqueur
¼ cup whipping or heavy cream, heated to boiling

*Use 1 cup whole blanched almonds, toasted, instead of hazelnuts, if desired.

Preheat oven to 325°F. Grease 9-inch cake pan and line bottom with parchment or waxed paper; set aside.

In food processor or blender, process hazelnuts and ¼ cup sugar until nuts are finely ground; set aside.

In top of double boiler, melt I Can't Believe It's Not Butter!® Spread and 10 squares chocolate over medium heat, stirring occasionally, until smooth; set aside and let cool.

In large bowl, with electric mixer, beat eggs and remaining ½ cup sugar until thick and pale yellow, about 4 minutes. Beat in chocolate mixture and espresso. Stir in hazelnut mixture. Pour into prepared pan.

Bake 30 minutes or until toothpick inserted in center comes out with moist crumbs. On wire rack, cool 10 minutes; remove from pan and cool completely.

In small bowl, pour hot cream over remaining 2 squares chocolate, chopped. Stir until chocolate is melted and mixture is smooth. Pour chocolate mixture over torte to glaze. Let stand at room temperature or refrigerate until chocolate mixture is set, about 30 minutes.   *Makes 8 servings*

Note: Torte may be frozen up to 1 month.

Chocolate Hazelnut Torte

Ginger Polenta Cookies

2¼ cups all-purpose flour
½ cup instant polenta or yellow cornmeal
½ cup toasted pistachio nuts or pine nuts, finely chopped
½ cup dried cranberries, finely chopped
   Pinch of salt
 1 cup (2 sticks) unsalted butter, softened
¾ cup sugar
 1 egg plus 1 yolk
½ cup crystallized ginger, finely chopped
½ teaspoon ground ginger

1. Combine flour, polenta, pistachio nuts, cranberries and salt in medium bowl; set aside.

2. Beat butter and sugar in large bowl with electric mixer at medium speed until light and fluffy. Beat in egg, yolk, chopped ginger and ground ginger. Add flour mixture; mix at low speed until well blended.

3. Gather dough into ball; divide in half. Shape into 2 (9-inch) logs; wrap in plastic wrap, sealing ends. Roll logs to smooth surface, if necessary. Refrigerate 4 to 6 hours or until firm.

4. Preheat oven to 300°F. Line cookie sheets with parchment paper. Cut logs into ¼-inch slices; place cookies on prepared cookie sheets. Bake 15 to 18 minutes or until edges are golden brown. Cool 2 to 3 minutes on cookie sheet; transfer to wire rack to cool completely.

Makes about 60 cookies

Cappuccino Cooler

1½ cups cold coffee
1½ cups chocolate ice cream
 ¼ cup HERSHEY'S Syrup
   Crushed ice
   Whipped cream
   Ground cinnamon (optional)

Combine coffee, ice cream and syrup in blender container. Cover; blend until smooth. Serve immediately over crushed ice. Garnish with whipped cream and cinnamon, if desired.

Makes about 4 servings

Variation: Substitute vanilla ice cream for chocolate; increase syrup to ⅓ cup.

Gramma's Cannoli Cassata

     6 cups whipping cream
     2 eggs
     1 cup sugar
     1 cup all-purpose flour
     1 teaspoon grated lemon peel
     ½ cup finely chopped dried fruit
     ½ cup ricotta cheese
     ½ cup rum
     ¼ cup chopped pecans
     2 teaspoons vanilla
     1 prepared pound cake (about 16 ounces), cut into ½-inch cubes

1. Whisk cream and eggs in medium saucepan just until blended. Whisk in sugar, flour and lemon peel until blended. Cook over medium heat about 5 to 10 minutes, stirring constantly, until mixture begins to thicken. *Do not boil.* Remove from heat; stir in dried fruit, ricotta, rum, pecans and vanilla.

2. Place one-third cake cubes in trifle dish, distributing pieces to cover bottom. Top with one-third cream mixture. Repeat layers twice, ending with cream mixture. Cover with plastic wrap; refrigerate at least 4 hours or overnight. Garnish as desired. Serve cold.   *Makes 12 servings*

Chocolate-Amaretto Ice

     ¾ cup sugar
     ½ cup HERSHEY'S Cocoa
     2 cups (1 pint) light cream or half-and-half
     2 tablespoons Amaretto (almond-flavored liqueur)
       Sliced almonds (optional)

1. Stir together sugar and cocoa in small saucepan; gradually stir in light cream. Cook over low heat, stirring constantly, until sugar dissolves and mixture is smooth and hot. Do not boil.

2. Remove from heat; stir in liqueur. Pour into 8-inch square pan. Cover; freeze until firm, stirring several times before mixture freezes. Scoop into dessert dishes; garnish with sliced almonds, if desired. Serve immediately.   *Makes 4 servings*

Hazelnut Biscotti

   6 hazelnuts
   ¼ cup sugar
   2 tablespoons butter
   2 egg whites, lightly beaten
1½ teaspoons vanilla
1½ cups all-purpose flour
   ½ teaspoon baking powder
   ½ teaspoon grated orange peel
   ⅛ teaspoon salt

1. Preheat oven to 375°F. Place hazelnuts in shallow baking pan; toast 7 to 8 minutes or until rich golden brown. Set aside. *Reduce oven temperature to 325°F.* Spray cookie sheet with nonstick cooking spray; set aside.

2. Combine sugar and butter in medium bowl; mix well. Add egg whites and vanilla; mix well. Combine flour, baking powder, orange peel and salt in large bowl; mix well. Finely chop toasted hazelnuts; stir into flour mixture. Add butter mixture to flour mixture; blend well.

3. Divide dough in half. Shape half of dough into log on lightly floured surface. (Dough will be soft.) Transfer to prepared cookie sheet. Repeat with remaining half of dough to form second log. Bake logs 25 minutes or until toothpick inserted into center of logs comes out clean. Cool on wire racks. *Reduce oven temperature to 300°F.*

4. When cool enough to handle, cut each log into 8 (½-inch) slices. Place, cut sides up, on cookie sheets. Bake slices 12 minutes. Turn; bake additional 12 minutes or until golden brown.

Makes 16 servings

BelGioioso® Mascarpone au Café

8 ounces BELGIOIOSO® Mascarpone
2 cups espresso coffee
2 tablespoons sugar
2 tablespoons brandy
1 package ladyfingers
   Sprinkles of bitter cocoa
1 cup ground nuts

Combine BelGioioso Mascarpone, ½ cup espresso coffee, sugar and brandy in large bowl. Soak ladyfingers in remaining 1½ cups espresso coffee (add more if necessary) mixed with a little additional brandy; place in a serving bowl. Alternate layers of ladyfingers and cream mixture, then sprinkle with cocoa and ground nuts. Refrigerate for 2 hours before serving.   *Makes 4 servings*

Hazelnut Biscotti

Chocolate Espresso Panini

2 tablespoons chocolate hazelnut spread
¼ teaspoon instant espresso powder
2 slices rustic Italian bread
  Nonstick cooking spray

1. Preheat indoor grill.* Combine chocolate spread and espresso powder in small bowl; mix well. Spread chocolate mixture evenly over one slice bread; top with second slice.

2. Spray sandwich lightly with nonstick cooking spray. Grill 2 to 3 minutes or until bread is golden brown.   *Makes 1 panini*

*Panini can also be made on the stove in a ridged grill pan or in a nonstick skillet. Cook sandwich over medium heat about 2 minutes per side.

Fig and Hazelnut Cake

¾ cup hazelnuts (about 4 ounces) with skins removed, coarsely chopped
¾ cup whole dried figs (about 4 ounces), coarsely chopped
⅔ cup slivered blanched almonds (about 3 ounces), coarsely chopped
3 squares (1 ounce each) semisweet chocolate, finely chopped
⅓ cup diced candied orange peel
⅓ cup diced candied lemon peel
1¼ cups all-purpose flour
1¾ teaspoons baking powder
¾ teaspoon salt
3 eggs
½ cup sugar

1. Preheat oven to 300°F. Grease 8×4-inch loaf pan; set aside. Combine hazelnuts, figs, almonds, chocolate and candied peels in medium bowl; mix well. Combine flour, baking powder and salt in small bowl.

2. Beat eggs and sugar in large bowl 5 minutes with electric mixer at high speed until thick and pale yellow. Gently fold nut mixture into egg mixture. Sift half of flour mixture over egg mixture; gently fold in. Repeat with remaining flour mixture.

3. Spread batter evenly into prepared pan. Bake 60 to 70 minutes or until top is golden brown and firm to the touch. Cool in pan on wire rack 5 minutes. Remove loaf from pan; cool completely on wire rack at least 4 hours.   *Makes 12 servings*

Chocolate Espresso Panini

Italian Ice

1 cup sugar
1 cup sweet or dry fruity white wine
1 cup water
1 cup lemon juice
2 egg whites*
Fresh berries (optional)

*Use pasteurized or clean, uncracked grade A eggs.

1. Combine sugar, wine and water in small saucepan. Cook over medium-high heat until sugar is dissolved and syrup boils, stirring frequently. Cover; boil 1 minute. Uncover; adjust heat to maintain simmer. Simmer 10 minutes without stirring. Remove from heat. Refrigerate 1 hour or until syrup is completely cool.

2. Stir lemon juice into cooled syrup. Pour into 9-inch round cake pan. Freeze 1 hour.

3. Quickly stir mixture with fork breaking up ice crystals. Freeze 1 hour more or until firm but not solid. Meanwhile, place medium bowl in freezer to chill.

4. Beat egg whites in small bowl with electric mixer at high speed until stiff peaks form. Remove lemon mixture from pan to chilled bowl. Immediately beat lemon mixture with whisk or fork until smooth. Fold in egg whites; mix well. Spread egg mixture evenly into same pan. Freeze 30 minutes. Immediately stir with fork; cover pan with foil. Freeze at least 3 hours or until firm.

5. Scoop ice into fluted champagne glasses or dessert dishes. Serve with berries.

Makes 4 servings

Italian Ice

Panettone Cake with Almond Glaze and Mascarpone Cream

½ **cup pine nuts**
½ **cup golden raisins**
½ **cup currants**
1 **cup warm water, divided**
1 **package (about 18 ounces) lemon cake mix, plus ingredients to prepare mix**
1½ **teaspoons anise seeds**
1 **cup ricotta cheese**
½ **cup mascarpone cheese**
¼ **cup granulated sugar**
⅔ **cup powdered sugar**
1 **tablespoon milk**
1 **teaspoon almond or anise extract**

1. To prepare cake, preheat oven to 325°F. Grease and flour 10-inch bundt pan; set aside.

2. Place pine nuts in small nonstick skillet over medium heat. Cook and stir 4 minutes until nuts are fragrant and lightly browned. Transfer to plate to cool; set aside.

3. Place raisins and currants in 2 separate small bowls. Add ½ cup warm water to each bowl; let fruit soak 5 minutes. Drain raisins and currants.

4. Prepare cake according to package directions, using only half of water called for. Stir in anise seeds, pine nuts, raisins and currants. Pour batter into prepared pan. Bake about 40 minutes or until top is golden brown and toothpick inserted near center comes out clean. Cool cake in pan on wire rack about 30 minutes.

5. Meanwhile, to prepare Mascarpone Cream, beat ricotta, mascarpone and granulated sugar in medium bowl 1 minute on low speed of electric mixer or until light and fluffy. Cover and refrigerate.

6. To prepare glaze, stir together powdered sugar, milk and almond extract in small bowl until smooth. Add more milk, ½ teaspoon at a time, until desired consistency.

7. Place sheets of waxed paper under wire rack. Spoon glaze over cake; let glaze set 20 minutes. Serve cake slices with Mascarpone Cream.

Makes 10 servings

Panettone Cake with Almond Glaze and Mascarpone Cream

Almond Amaretto Loaf

1 cup milk
1 egg
2 tablespoons butter or margarine, softened
¼ cup amaretto liqueur
1 teaspoon lemon juice
¾ teaspoon salt
3 cups bread flour
½ cup chopped almonds, toasted
¼ cup sugar
2 teaspoons FLEISCHMANN'S® Bread Machine Yeast
   Amaretto Glaze (recipe follows)
¼ cup sliced almonds, toasted

Add all ingredients except glaze and sliced almonds to bread machine pan in the order suggested by manufacturer, adding chopped almonds with flour. (If dough is too dry or stiff, or too soft or slack, adjust dough consistency). Recommended cycle: Basic/white bread cycle; light or medium/normal crust color setting. *Do not use delay cycle.*

Remove bread from pan; cool on wire rack. Drizzle with Amaretto Glaze and sprinkle with sliced almonds. *Makes 1 (½-pound) loaf*

Amaretto Glaze: Combine 1 cup powdered sugar, sifted, 2 tablespoons amaretto liqueur and enough milk (1 to 2 teaspoons) to make glaze of drizzling consistency.

Almond Amaretto Loaf

Custard Rum Torta

6 eggs
1¼ cups granulated sugar, divided
¾ teaspoon salt, divided
1¼ cups all-purpose flour
⅓ cup cornstarch
3½ cups milk
2 egg yolks
2 tablespoons butter
2 teaspoons vanilla
2 pints fresh strawberries
6 tablespoons dark rum
4 cups (2 pints) heavy or whipping cream
¼ cup powdered sugar, sifted

1. For cake, preheat oven to 350°F. Grease and flour 10-inch springform pan. Beat eggs in large bowl with electric mixer at high speed until foamy. Add ¾ cup granulated sugar, 2 tablespoons at a time, beating well after each addition. Beat 3 minutes more. Beat in ¼ teaspoon salt. Sift one-third flour over egg mixture; fold in. Repeat until all flour has been incorporated.

2. Spread batter into prepared pan. Bake 40 minutes or until toothpick inserted into center comes out clean. Cool in pan on wire rack 10 minutes. Loosen side of pan from cake; remove. Remove cake from bottom of pan to wire rack. Cool completely. Clean pan.

3. For custard, combine remaining ½ cup granulated sugar, cornstarch and remaining ½ teaspoon salt in large saucepan; mix well. Stir in milk until smooth. Bring to a boil over medium heat, stirring frequently. Boil 3 minutes, stirring constantly; remove from heat. Whisk egg yolks in small bowl; gradually whisk in 1 cup hot milk mixture. Gradually whisk egg yolk mixture into remaining milk mixture in saucepan. Cook over low heat 1 minute, stirring constantly. Immediately pour custard into medium bowl. Cut butter into pieces; add to custard and stir until melted. Stir in vanilla. Press waxed paper onto surface of custard; refrigerate. Cool completely.

4. Reserve 8 whole strawberries for garnish. Hull and thinly slice remaining strawberries.

5. Cut cake horizontally into 3 layers using long serrated knife. To assemble torta, brush top of each cake layer with 2 tablespoons rum. Place one cake layer in bottom of springform pan. Spread with half of custard. Arrange half of strawberry slices over custard in single layer. Top with second cake layer; spread with remaining custard and top with remaining strawberry slices. Place third cake layer on top. Cover and refrigerate at least 12 hours.

6. About 45 minutes before serving, beat cream with powdered sugar in large bowl with electric mixer at high speed until stiff. Spoon 2 cups whipped cream mixture into pastry bag fitted with large star tip; refrigerate. Remove side of pan; place torta on serving plate (do not remove bottom of pan). Spread remaining whipped cream mixture on sides and top of torte. Pipe reserved whipped cream mixture around top and bottom edges. Refrigerate 30 minutes before serving. Garnish with reserved whole strawberries. *Makes 10 to 12 servings*

Orange-Thyme Granita in Cookie Cups

2½ cups fresh orange juice
½ cup fresh lemon juice
¼ cup sugar
1 teaspoon finely chopped fresh thyme
6 Lemon Anise Cookie Cups (recipe follows)
Fresh mint leaves (optional)
Lemon peel (optional)

1. Combine juices, sugar and thyme in medium bowl; stir until sugar dissolves. Freeze about 1 hour or until slightly firm. Beat with wire whisk to break ice crystals. Repeat freezing and beating 2 to 3 times until ice is firm and granular.

2. Meanwhile, prepare Lemon-Anise Cookie Cups. To serve, scoop ½ cup granita into each cookie cup. Garnish with mint and lemon peel. *Makes 6 servings*

Lemon-Anise Cookie Cups

3 tablespoons all-purpose flour
3 tablespoons sugar
2 tablespoons butter, melted
1 egg white
1 teaspoon grated lemon peel
¼ teaspoon anise extract
¼ cup sliced almonds

1. Preheat oven to 375°F. Combine flour, sugar, butter, egg white, lemon peel and anise extract in food processor; process until smooth. Spray outside of 6 custard cups and 2 baking sheets with nonstick cooking spray. Spread 1 tablespoon batter into 5-inch-diameter circle on baking sheet with rubber spatula. Repeat to make total of 6 circles. Sprinkle 2 teaspoons almonds in center of each.

2. Bake 3 to 4 minutes or until edges are browned. Place each cookie over bottom of prepared custard cup so almonds face inside. Press against custard cup to form cookie cups. Cool completely. *Makes 6 cookie cups*

Orange-Thyme Granita in Cookie Cup

Tiramisù

2 packages (3 ounces each) ladyfingers, thawed if frozen, split in half horizontally
¾ cup brewed espresso*
2 tablespoons coffee liqueur or brandy (optional)
1 package (8 ounces) cream cheese, softened
2 tablespoons sugar
⅓ cup sour cream
½ cup whipping cream
2 tablespoons unsweetened cocoa powder, divided

Use fresh brewed espresso, instant espresso powder prepared according to directions on jar or 2 teaspoons instant coffee powder dissolved in ¾ cup hot water.

1. Place ladyfingers on baking sheet. Let stand, uncovered, 8 hours or overnight to dry. Or dry ladyfingers by placing on microwavable plate. Microwave on MEDIUM-HIGH (70%) 1 minute, turn ladyfingers over. Microwave on MEDIUM-HIGH 1 to 1½ minutes or until dry.

2. Combine espresso and liqueur, if desired, in small bowl. Dip half the ladyfingers in espresso mixture; place in bottom of 2-quart serving bowl.

3. Beat cream cheese and sugar with electric mixer at medium speed until fluffy; add sour cream, beating until blended. Add whipping cream, beating until smooth. Spread half the cheese mixture over ladyfingers.

4. Place 1 tablespoon cocoa in fine strainer. Lightly dust cocoa over cheese layer.

5. Dip remaining ladyfingers in espresso mixture. Place over cheese mixture in serving bowl.

6. Spread remaining cheese mixture over ladyfingers. Dust remaining 1 tablespoon cocoa over cheese layer. Refrigerate, covered, 4 hours or overnight. Garnish with chocolate curls and mint leaves, if desired.
Makes 6 servings

Zabaglione

5 egg yolks
¼ cup sugar
½ cup sweet marsala wine, divided
¼ cup dry white wine

1. Place egg yolks in top of double boiler; add sugar. Beat with electric mixer at medium speed until pale yellow and creamy. Place water in bottom of double boiler. Bring to a boil over high heat; reduce heat to low. Place top of double boiler over hot water. Gradually beat ¼ cup marsala into egg yolk mixture. Beat 1 minute. Gradually beat in remaining ¼ cup marsala and white wine.

continued on page 246

 2. Cook 6 to 10 minutes until mixture is fluffy and thick enough to form soft mounds when dropped from beaters, beating constantly and scraping bottom and side of pan frequently. (Do not overcook or custard will curdle.) Remove top of double boiler from water. Whisk custard briefly. Pour into 4 individual serving dishes; serve immediately. *Makes 4 servings*

Rustic Honey Polenta Cake

2½ cups all-purpose flour
1 cup yellow cornmeal
2 tablespoons baking powder
1 teaspoon salt
1 cup (2 sticks) butter or margarine, melted
1¾ cups milk
¾ cup honey
2 eggs, slightly beaten
Honey-Orange Syrup (recipe follows)
Sweetened whipped cream and orange segments for garnish (optional)

In large bowl, combine flour, cornmeal, baking powder and salt; mix well. In small bowl, combine melted butter, milk, honey and eggs; mix well. Stir into flour mixture, mixing until just blended. Pour into lightly greased 13×9-inch baking pan.

Bake at 325°F for 25 to 30 minutes or until toothpick comes out clean. Meanwhile, prepare Honey-Orange Syrup. When cake is done, remove from oven to wire rack. Pour hot syrup evenly over top of cake, spreading if necessary to cover entire surface. Cool completely. Garnish with dollop of whipped cream and orange segments, if desired. *Makes 12 servings*

Honey-Orange Syrup: In small saucepan, whisk together ½ cup honey, 3 tablespoons orange juice concentrate and 1 tablespoon freshly grated orange peel. Heat over medium-high heat until mixture begins to boil; remove from heat.

Favorite recipe from **National Honey Board**

The publisher would like to thank the companies and organizations listed below for the use of their recipes and photographs in this publication.

ACH Food Companies, Inc.

American Lamb Council

Bays English Muffin Corporation

BelGioioso® Cheese Inc.

California Olive Industry

Cucina Classica Italiana, Inc.

Del Monte Corporation

Dole Food Company, Inc.

Filippo Berio® Olive Oil

The Hershey Company

Holland House® is a registered trademark of Mott's, LLP

Lucini Italia Co.

Mushroom Council

National Cattlemen's Beef Association on Behalf of The Beef Checkoff

National Fisheries Institute

National Honey Board

National Pork Board

National Turkey Federation

Nestlé USA

Newman's Own, Inc.®

Norseland, Inc.

Perdue Farms Incorporated

Reckitt Benckiser Inc.

RED STAR® Yeast, a product of Lasaffre Yeast Corporation

Sargento® Foods Inc.

StarKist® Tuna

Unilever

USA Rice FederationTM

Wisconsin Milk Marketing Board

METRIC CONVERSION CHART

VOLUME MEASUREMENTS (dry)

$^1/_8$ teaspoon = 0.5 mL
$^1/_4$ teaspoon = 1 mL
$^1/_2$ teaspoon = 2 mL
$^3/_4$ teaspoon = 4 mL
1 teaspoon = 5 mL
1 tablespoon = 15 mL
2 tablespoons = 30 mL
$^1/_4$ cup = 60 mL
$^1/_3$ cup = 75 mL
$^1/_2$ cup = 125 mL
$^2/_3$ cup = 150 mL
$^3/_4$ cup = 175 mL
1 cup = 250 mL
2 cups = 1 pint = 500 mL
3 cups = 750 mL
4 cups = 1 quart = 1 L

VOLUME MEASUREMENTS (fluid)

1 fluid ounce (2 tablespoons) = 30 mL
4 fluid ounces ($^1/_2$ cup) = 125 mL
8 fluid ounces (1 cup) = 250 mL
12 fluid ounces (1$^1/_2$ cups) = 375 mL
16 fluid ounces (2 cups) = 500 mL

WEIGHTS (mass)

$^1/_2$ ounce = 15 g
1 ounce = 30 g
3 ounces = 90 g
4 ounces = 120 g
8 ounces = 225 g
10 ounces = 285 g
12 ounces = 360 g
16 ounces = 1 pound = 450 g

DIMENSIONS

$^1/_{16}$ inch = 2 mm
$^1/_8$ inch = 3 mm
$^1/_4$ inch = 6 mm
$^1/_2$ inch = 1.5 cm
$^3/_4$ inch = 2 cm
1 inch = 2.5 cm

OVEN TEMPERATURES

250°F = 120°C
275°F = 140°C
300°F = 150°C
325°F = 160°C
350°F = 180°C
375°F = 190°C
400°F = 200°C
425°F = 220°C
450°F = 230°C

BAKING PAN SIZES

Utensil	Size in Inches/Quarts	Metric Volume	Size in Centimeters
Baking or Cake Pan (square or rectangular)	8×8×2	2 L	20×20×5
	9×9×2	2.5 L	23×23×5
	12×8×2	3 L	30×20×5
	13×9×2	3.5 L	33×23×5
Loaf Pan	8×4×3	1.5 L	20×10×7
	9×5×3	2 L	23×13×7
Round Layer Cake Pan	8×1½	1.2 L	20×4
	9×1½	1.5 L	23×4
Pie Plate	8×1¼	750 mL	20×3
	9×1¼	1 L	23×3
Baking Dish or Casserole	1 quart	1 L	—
	1½ quart	1.5 L	—
	2 quart	2 L	—